# easy microwave menus

microwave cooking library®

by barbara methven

microwave cooking library®

Planning meals is both a science and an art. You need to consider balanced nutrition, flavor combinations, the interplay of contrasting textures and temperatures, as well as visual appeal. You want to produce this nutritious, appealing meal with a minimum of time and effort. Few people have the leisure to spend all day preparing a meal, even if they wanted to.

*Easy Microwave Menus* does the work of planning for you.

Here's a book full of exciting menus for everyday and company meals, with all the recipes you need to prepare each one conveniently, following the appropriate menu. Step-by-step guides help you manage your time efficiently, so preparation is quick and easy. You'll find that fresh variety in your menus makes mealtime more interesting and cooking more fun.

*Barbara Methven*

Barbara Methven

CREDITS:
*Design & Production:* Cy DeCosse Incorporated
*Senior Art Director:* David Schelitzche
*Art Directors:* Rebecca Gammelgaard, Lisa Rosenthal
*Project Managers:* Lynette Reber, Ann Schlachter
*Home Economists:* Peggy Ramette, Ann Stuart, Ginny Hoeschen, Kathy Weber, Grace Wells
*Consultants:* Ginny Hoeschen, Kathleen Schutte, Grace Wells
*Recipe Editor:* Janice Cauley
*Production Manager:* Jim Bindas
*Assistant Production Managers:* Julie Churchill, Jacquie Marx
*Typesetting:* Kevin D. Frakes, Linda Schloegel
*Production Staff:* Russell Beaver, Holly Clements, Sheila DiPaola, Joe Fahey, Yelena Konrardy, Scott Lamoureux, Bob Lynch, Jody Phillips, Greg Wallace, Nik Wogstad
*Studio Manager:* Cathleen Shannon
*Photographers:* Rex Irmen, Tony Kubat, John Lauenstein, Bill Lindner, Mark Macemon, Mette Nielsen
*Food Stylists:* Melinda Hutchison, Amy Peterson, Sue Sinon, Ann Stuart
*Contributing Food Stylists:* Suzanne Finley, Susan Zechmann
*Color Separations:* Spectrum, Inc.
*Printing:* R. R. Donnelley & Sons (0389)

CY DE COSSE INCORPORATED
*Chairman:* Cy DeCosse
*President:* James B. Maus
*Executive Vice President:* William B. Jones

Library of Congress Cataloging-in-Publication Data.

Methven, Barbara.
Easy Microwave Menus

(Microwave cooking library)

Includes index.
1. Microwave cookery. I. Title. II. Series.
TX832.M392 1989 641.5'882 88-30911
ISBN 0-86573-560-3
ISBN 0-86573-561-1 (pbk.)

# Contents

**Thai Dinner**

Bangkok Shrimp Sauté

Vegetables in Ginger Butter

Fresh Pineapple Sorbet

Sesame Pasta

# What You Need to Know Before You Start

"What's for dinner?" Answering that question, day after day, challenges the imagination. Add breakfasts, lunches and dinner parties, and meal planning can consume more time than you have to devote to it.

Use this versatile collection of menus and recipes as a step-by-step guide or as an idea book to stimulate your own creativity. The recipes you need for each meal follow the menu, so you don't have to shift from one section of the book to another as you cook the foods. You use the microwave oven, the conventional oven and cooktop to prepare a variety of foods quickly. Time management guides help make preparation easy so you get everything ready to serve at the same time.

## Family Fare

These menus for breakfast, lunch and dinner reflect a contemporary taste for interesting, light and nonfussy meals. The menus limit preparation to two or three recipes. An asterisk after a menu item, such as Assorted Pickles* or Tossed Salad with Bottled Dressing*, indicates that no recipe is needed. No desserts are suggested for these menus. If your family prefers a daily dessert, offer fresh fruit or ice cream, or prepare a favorite recipe or mix.

## Entertaining

Menus for entertaining offer a greater variety of foods and more side dishes than the family meals. Each menu is planned around a theme and serves six to eight people. All of the desserts are made the day before. You can also prepare many other menu items partly or completely in advance.

Dividing preparation into several manageable segments makes it possible for a working host or hostess to entertain without last-minute pressure.

## At-A-Glance Alternatives

As a source of new ideas, the menus suggest foods, flavor combinations or preparation techniques that you can adapt to your own taste and needs. If you like a main dish but would prefer a different accompaniment, substitute another recipe. To make choosing alternatives easy, pages 6 to 11 present color photographs of all the *salad, vegetable* and *dessert* recipes, with the number of servings and page numbers printed below them.

## Nutritional Information

Following every recipe you'll find a per serving analysis of the calorie, protein, carbohydrate, fat, sodium and cholesterol content. Where serving quantity varies, the analysis is for the greater number of servings. For example, if a main dish serves six to eight people, the nutritional analysis is based on eight servings. Where a recipe suggests alternative ingredients, such as margarine or butter, the analysis applies to the first ingredient listed. Substituting the alternative ingredient may alter the nutritional analysis.

# Side Salads

The choice of salads includes mixed greens, vegetable or fruit combinations, gelatins and a frozen salad. Choose a different dressing, make your own secret recipe, or for convenience, use bottled dressing.

**Spinach-Apple Salad**
Serves 4-6                    Page 51

**Tomato, Provolone & Red Onion Salad**
Serves 4-6                    Page 57

**Chinese Coleslaw**
Serves 4-6                    Page 66

**Fresh Strawberry-Banana Salad**
Serves 4-6                    Page 69

**Southwestern Salad**
Serves 4-6                    Page 73

**Mandarin Orange Gelatin Squares**
Serves 9                    Page 77

**Light Green Salad with Oil & Vinegar Dressing**
Serves 4-6                    Page 85

**Light Green Salad with Cucumber-Dill Dressing**
Serves 4-6                    Page 87

**Frozen Fruit Salad**
Serves 8-16                    Page 108

**Apple Crunch Salad**
Serves 8                       Page 112

**Homegrown Tomato & Cucumber Salad**
Serves 6                       Page 116

**Jicama Salad with Lime-Honey Dressing**
Serves 6                       Page 121

**Romaine Salad with Parmesan Peppercorn Dressing**
Serves 6-8                     Page 126

**Pear & Walnut Salad**
Serves 6                       Page 134

**Oriental Pasta & Vegetable Salad**
Serves 6-8                     Page 138

**New Potato & Avocado Salad**
Serves 6-8                     Page 142

**Caribbean Cabbage Salad**
Serves 8                       Page 148

# Vegetables

When choosing an alternative vegetable, look for one whose color, texture and flavor complements the main dish and other accompaniments. Read the recipes for your revised menu and adjust the time management, if necessary.

**Basiled New Potatoes**
Serves 4-6                    Page 47

**Marinated Summer Vegetables**
Serves 4-6                    Page 47

**Carrot & Squash Ribbons**
Serves 4-6                    Page 49

**Gingered Orange-glazed Carrots**
Serves 4-6                    Page 53

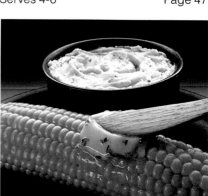

**Honey-buttered Corn**
Serves 4                    Page 55

**Baked Potatoes**
Serves 6                    Page 62

**Garden Favorites**
Serves 4-6                    Page 70

**Jalapeño Cheddar Potatoes**
Serves 4-6                    Page 73

**Broccoli Spears with Mustard Sauce**
Serves 4-6                    Page 75

**Apple-buttered Brussels Sprouts**
Serves 4-6                    Page 78

**Black-eyed Peas & Peppers**
Serves 4-6                    Page 81

**Rosemary-buttered Summer Squash**
Serves 4-6                    Page 82

**Summer Vegetable Medley**
Serves 4-6                    Page 83

**Tri-colored Peppers**
Serves 6-8                    Page 99

**Zucchini Strips with Cilantro Butter**
Serves 6-8                    Page 101

**Oven-browned Potatoes**
Serves 6-8                    Page 107

**Bean & Carrot Amandine**
Serves 6-8                    Page 107

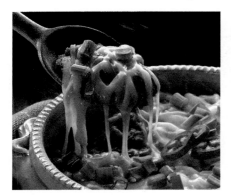
**Cheese-topped Refried Beans**
Serves 6                      Page 122

**Sunny Artichoke Platter**
Serves 8                      Page 129

**Alfredo Spaghetti Squash**
Serves 6                      Page 133

**Tropical Sweet Potato & Pineapple Kabobs**
Serves 8                      Page 146

**Vegetables in Ginger Butter**
Serves 6                      Page 150

# Desserts

Since all the desserts in this book are prepared in advance, a substitution will not affect the preparation schedule. Choose a delicate, tart or refreshing dessert to follow rich foods or an extensive menu. Complement a light meal with small portions of a sumptuous dessert.

**Pink Lemonade Dessert Squares**
Serves 12                    Page 93

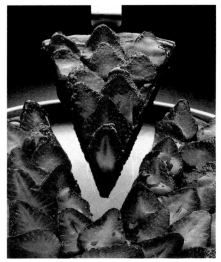

**Strawberry Brownie Tart**
Serves 12                    Page 96

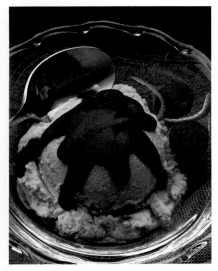

**Frozen Yogurt & Lime-Raspberry Sauce**
Serves 16                    Page 99

**Rainbow Ice Cream Terrine**
Serves 12                    Page 101

**Upside-down Peach Praline Pie**
Serves 8                     Page 104

**Glazed Apple Spice Cake**
Serves 12                    Page 109

**Lemon Pudding Cake**
Serves 8-10                  Page 113

**Mixed Fall Fruit Crisp**
Serves 6-8                   Page 117

**Orange Rum Soufflés**
Serves 6                    Page 123

**Spumoni Cake**
Serves 12                   Page 126

**Petite Croissants with Fresh Fruit & French Crème**
Serves 12                   Page 131

**Decadent Chocolate Torte**
Serves 12                   Page 135

**Almond Cookies**
Serves 24                   Page 139

**Blueberry Sugar-crusted Cobbler**
Serves 8                    Page 143

**Mint Chip Cheesecake**
Serves 12                   Page 145

**Coconut Cream Parfaits**
Serves 8                    Page 149

**Fresh Pineapple Sorbet**
Serves 8                    Page 152

# Quick Breakfasts

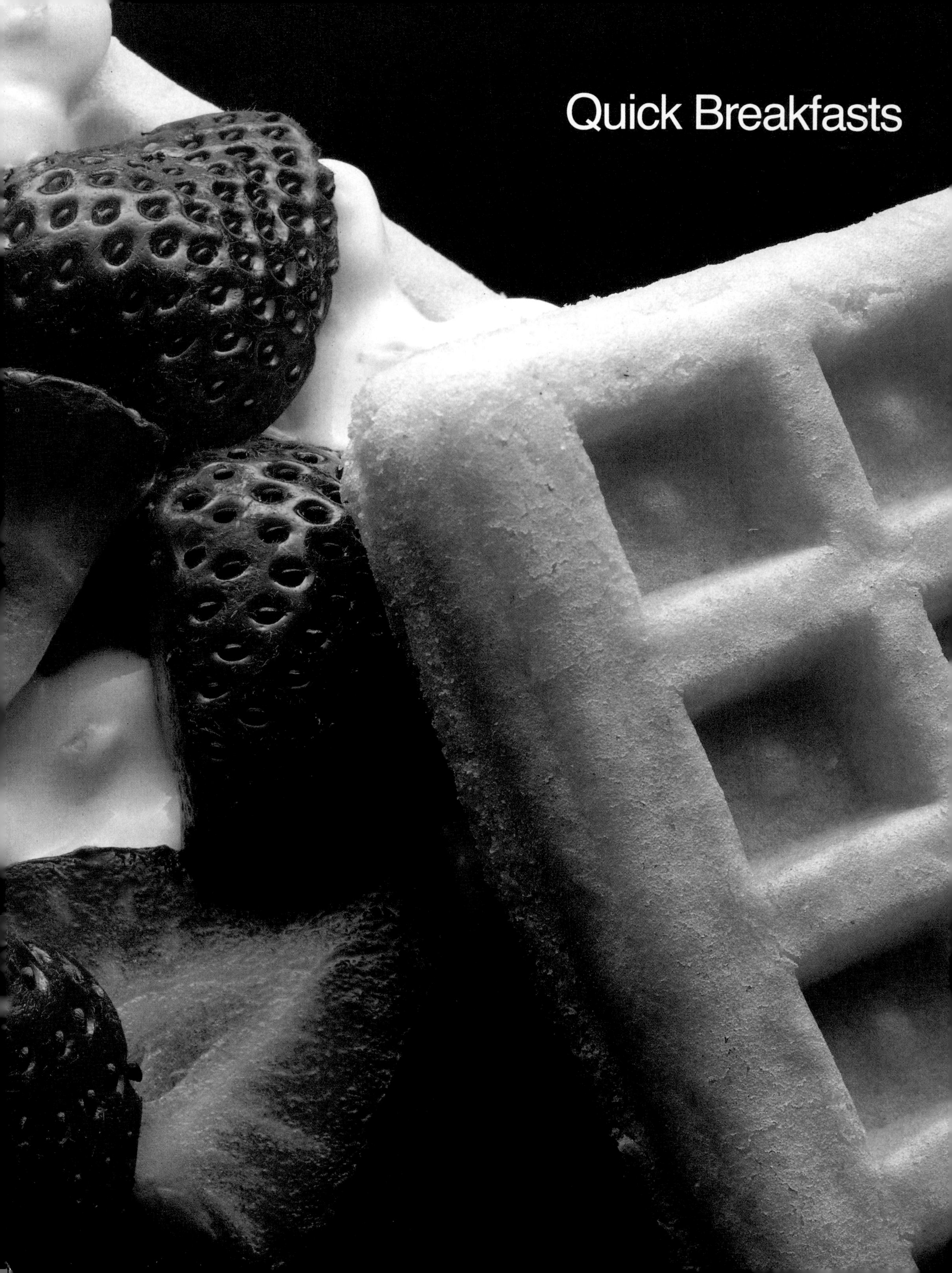

## Denver Burrito

### Time Management

- Chop vegetables and microwave. • Chop ham; add to vegetables with eggs and seasoning. • Microwave egg mixture. Sprinkle with cheese; let stand. • Soften tortilla. Fill, roll and top with salsa.

¼ cup chopped green pepper
1 tablespoon chopped onion
1 tablespoon salsa
2 eggs
¼ cup chopped fully cooked ham (optional)

Dash garlic salt
Dash dried red pepper flakes
2 tablespoons shredded Cheddar cheese
1 flour tortilla (10-inch)

1 serving

In small mixing bowl, combine green pepper, onion and salsa. Cover with plastic wrap. Microwave at High for 1 to 1½ minutes, or until vegetables are tender-crisp. Add eggs, ham, garlic salt and red pepper flakes. Scramble eggs with fork. Microwave at High for 1¼ to 1¾ minutes, or until eggs are set but still moist, stirring twice to break up cooked portions. Sprinkle with cheese. Cover with plastic wrap. Set aside.

Place tortilla on plate between two dampened paper towels. Microwave at High for 10 to 15 seconds, or until tortilla is warm to the touch. Spoon egg mixture down center of tortilla. Roll up. Serve topped with additional salsa, if desired.

Per Serving:

| | | | |
|---|---|---|---|
| Calories: | 297 | Fat: | 17 g. |
| Protein: | 18 g. | Sodium: | 442 mg. |
| Carbohydrate: | 19 g. | Cholesterol: | 564 mg. |

*Old-fashioned Oatmeal
topped with
Apple Maple,
Caribbean Banana
or Spiced Peach*

*Juice\**

*Milk or Coffee\**

## Time Management

• Microwave oatmeal. • Prepare desired fruit topping. • Assemble and serve.

## Old-fashioned Oatmeal

⅓  cup old-fashioned rolled oats
¾  cup hot water
   Dash salt

1 serving

In 1-quart casserole, combine all ingredients. Microwave at High for 4 to 6 minutes, or until oatmeal thickens and is desired consistency, stirring twice.

Per Serving:
| | |
|---|---|
| Calories: | 103 |
| Protein: | 4 g. |
| Carbohydrate: | 18 g. |
| Fat: | 2 g. |
| Sodium: | 133 mg. |
| Cholesterol: | — |

## Apple Maple Oatmeal ▲

   Old-fashioned Oatmeal
   (above)
½  small apple, cut into chunks
1  tablespoon chopped walnuts
1  tablespoon maple syrup

1 serving

Prepare oatmeal as directed. Top oatmeal with apples and walnuts. Drizzle with maple syrup.

Per Serving:
| | |
|---|---|
| Calories: | 234 |
| Protein: | 5 g. |
| Carbohydrate: | 41 g. |
| Fat: | 7 g. |
| Sodium: | 136 mg. |
| Cholesterol: | — |

## Caribbean Banana Oatmeal

   Old-fashioned Oatmeal (left)
2  tablespoons flaked coconut
1  tablespoon packed brown sugar
1  tablespoon raisins
½  small banana, sliced

1 serving

Prepare oatmeal as directed. In small bowl, mix coconut, brown sugar and raisins. Top oatmeal with bananas. Sprinkle with coconut mixture.

Per Serving:
| | |
|---|---|
| Calories: | 280 |
| Protein: | 6 g. |
| Carbohydrate: | 56 g. |
| Fat: | 5 g. |
| Sodium: | 141 mg. |
| Cholesterol: | — |

## Spiced Peach Oatmeal

   Old-fashioned Oatmeal (left)
1  tablespoon packed brown sugar
⅛  teaspoon pumpkin pie spice
½  small peach, cut into chunks

1 serving

Prepare oatmeal as directed. In small bowl, mix brown sugar and pumpkin pie spice. Top oatmeal with peaches. Sprinkle with brown sugar mixture.

Per Serving:
| | |
|---|---|
| Calories: | 174 |
| Protein: | 5 g. |
| Carbohydrate: | 36 g. |
| Fat: | 2 g. |
| Sodium: | 137 mg. |
| Cholesterol: | — |

## Stuffed Fruit & Cheese Waffle

*MENU*

*Stuffed Fruit & Cheese Waffle*
*Milk, Coffee or Tea\**

### Time Management

• Slice fruit. • Microwave cream cheese to soften; stir in preserves. • Toast waffles conventionally. • Assemble.

2 oz. Neufchâtel or light cream
    cheese
1 tablespoon milk
1 tablespoon apricot or
    pineapple preserves or
    orange marmalade

2 frozen waffles
1 small nectarine, peach, apple
    or 4 to 6 strawberries, sliced

1 serving

In small bowl, microwave Neufchâtel at High for 15 to 20 seconds, or until softened. Stir in milk and the preserves. Set aside. Toast waffles or prepare in microwave as directed on package. Spread 1 tablespoon cheese mixture evenly on one side of one waffle. Top with two-thirds of fruit slices. Spoon 1 tablespoon of cheese mixture over fruit. Top with remaining waffle. Spoon remaining cheese mixture over top of waffle. Garnish with remaining fruit slices.

| Per Serving: | | | |
|---|---|---|---|
| Calories: | 394 | Fat: | 18 g. |
| Protein: | 11 g. | Sodium: | 597 mg. |
| Carbohydrate: | 50 g. | Cholesterol: | 114 mg. |

## MENU

*Granola Yogurt Bar*
*Juice**
*Coffee or Tea**

### Time Management

• Prepare Granola Yogurt Bars the day before serving. • In the morning, prepare juice and hot beverage.

## Granola Yogurt Bar

**Base:**
- ⅓ cup margarine or butter
- ⅓ cup packed dark brown sugar
- 2 tablespoons honey
- 1 teaspoon vanilla
- 1½ cups old-fashioned rolled oats
- ½ cup all-purpose flour
- ½ cup flaked coconut
- ⅓ cup chopped almonds

**Topping:**
- ¼ cup orange juice
- 1 teaspoon unflavored gelatin
- 4 oz. Neufchâtel or light cream cheese
- 1 carton (8 oz.) fruit-flavored low-fat yogurt
- ¼ cup flaked coconut

1 dozen bars

Heat conventional oven to 325°F. Grease 9-inch square baking pan. Set aside. In medium mixing bowl, microwave margarine at 30% (Medium Low) for 15 seconds to 1 minute, or until softened, checking every 15 seconds. Add brown sugar, honey and vanilla. Beat at medium speed of electric mixer until creamed. Stir in remaining base ingredients. Mix well. Press mixture into prepared pan. Bake for 18 to 20 minutes, or until golden brown. Cool completely.

Place orange juice in 1-cup measure. Stir in gelatin. Microwave at High for 45 seconds to 1 minute, or until gelatin is dissolved, stirring after 30 seconds. Set aside. Place cheese in small mixing bowl. Microwave at High for 30 to 45 seconds, or until softened. Add gelatin mixture and yogurt. Mix well. Pour evenly over cooled base. Sprinkle coconut in 9-inch pie plate. Microwave at High for 3 to 4 minutes, or until lightly browned, tossing with fork after the first minute and then every 30 seconds. Sprinkle coconut over yogurt mixture. Chill bars at least 2 hours, or until topping is set. Store, covered, in refrigerator.

| Per Serving: | | | |
|---|---|---|---|
| Calories: | 227 | Fat: | 12 g. |
| Protein: | 5 g. | Sodium: | 113 mg. |
| Carbohydrate: | 27 g. | Cholesterol: | 8 mg. |

## Pineapple Cheese Toast

### Time Management

• Toast French toast conventionally while you measure ingredients for syrup. • Spread cottage cheese on toast and top with pineapple. • Microwave syrup; pour over Pineapple Cheese Toast.

1 slice frozen French toast
2 tablespoons small-curd cottage cheese
1 canned pineapple slice

2 tablespoons packed dark brown sugar
2 teaspoons pineapple juice (reserved from can)
1 teaspoon margarine or butter

1 serving

Toast French toast or prepare in microwave as directed on package. Spread toast with cottage cheese. Top with pineapple slice. Set aside. In small bowl, combine brown sugar, pineapple juice and margarine. Microwave at High for 45 seconds to 1 minute, or until bubbly, stirring once. Pour over Pineapple Cheese Toast.

Per Serving:

| | | | |
|---|---|---|---|
| Calories: | 304 | Fat: | 9 g. |
| Protein: | 9 g. | Sodium: | 326 mg. |
| Carbohydrate: | 49 g. | Cholesterol: | 142 mg. |

*MENU*

---

*In-A-Hurry Health Drink*

---

**Time Management**

• Defrost fruit in microwave oven.
• Process all ingredients in blender. Serve.

## In-A-Hurry Health Drink

½ cup frozen sliced peaches,
　　　strawberries or blueberries
½ cup buttermilk
⅓ cup vanilla-flavored low-fat
　　　yogurt
1 egg white
2 tablespoons wheat germ
1 tablespoon honey

1 serving

In small mixing bowl, microwave fruit at High for 45 seconds to 1 minute, or until cold but not icy. Combine fruit and remaining ingredients in blender or food processor. Process until mixture is smooth and frothy. Serve immediately.

| Per Serving: | |
|---|---|
| Calories: | 325 |
| Protein: | 16 g. |
| Carbohydrate: | 61 g. |
| Fat: | 4 g. |
| Sodium: | 246 mg. |
| Cholesterol: | 8 mg. |

# Light Meals & Lunches

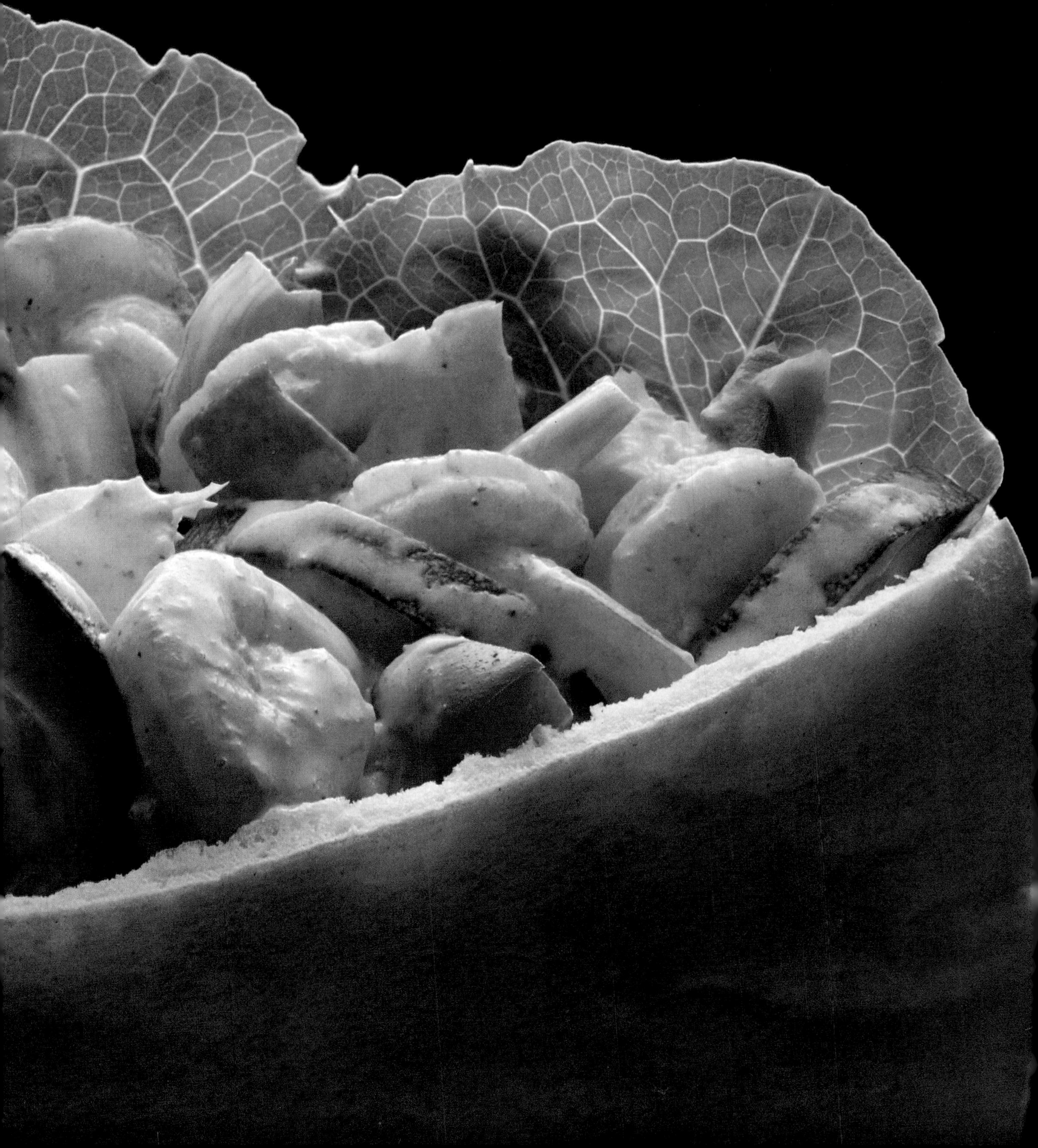

## ◄ Fiesta Soup

| | |
|---|---|
| 1 cup coarsely chopped onion | 1 jar (12 oz.) salsa |
| 1 cup chopped green pepper | 1 can (10¾ oz.) condensed tomato soup |
| 2 tablespoons olive oil | 1 can (8 oz.) corn, drained |
| 1½ teaspoons chili powder | 1 cup fully cooked julienne chicken (2 × ¼-inch strips) |
| 1 clove garlic, minced | |
| 1 can (14½ oz.) ready-to-serve chicken broth | |

4 to 6 servings

In 2-quart casserole, combine onion, green pepper, oil, chili powder and garlic. Cover. Microwave at High for 5 to 7 minutes, or until vegetables are tender, stirring once. Stir in remaining ingredients. Re-cover. Microwave at High for 7 to 9 minutes, or until soup is hot, stirring once or twice. Garnish with sour cream and sliced black olives, if desired.

Per Serving:

| | | | |
|---|---|---|---|
| Calories: | 189 | Fat: | 8 g. |
| Protein: | 10 g. | Sodium: | 1054 mg. |
| Carbohydrate: | 19 g. | Cholesterol: | 21 mg. |

## ◄ Seasoned Homemade Corn Chips

| | |
|---|---|
| 3 corn tortillas (6-inch) | Seasoned salt |
| 1 tablespoon vegetable oil | |

4 to 6 servings

Heat conventional oven to 400°F. Cut each tortilla into 6 wedges. Arrange in even layer on large baking sheet. Drizzle with oil. Sprinkle lightly with salt. Bake for 8 to 10 minutes, or until chips are crisp and light golden brown.

Per Serving:

| | | | |
|---|---|---|---|
| Calories: | 52 | Fat: | 3 g. |
| Protein: | 1 g. | Sodium: | 16 mg. |
| Carbohydrate: | 7 g. | Cholesterol: | — |

## Smoked Turkey & Vegetable Chowder

**Time Management**

• Heat conventional oven and start soup. • While soup microwaves, bake biscuits and prepare salad.

½ cup chopped red pepper
½ cup chopped green pepper
2 tablespoons margarine or butter
1 clove garlic, minced
¼ cup all-purpose flour
½ teaspoon salt
⅛ teaspoon dried thyme leaves
⅛ teaspoon pepper
1 can (14½ oz.) ready-to-serve chicken broth
1½ cups cubed smoked turkey (½-inch cubes)
1 pkg. (10 oz.) frozen corn
1½ cups half-and-half

4 to 6 servings

In 2-quart casserole, combine red pepper, green pepper, margarine and garlic. Cover. Microwave at High for 3 to 4 minutes, or until vegetables are tender-crisp. Stir in flour, salt, thyme and pepper. Blend in chicken broth. Add turkey and corn. Re-cover. Microwave at High for 13 to 20 minutes, or until mixture thickens and bubbles, stirring 3 times. Blend in half-and-half. Re-cover. Microwave at 50% (Medium) for 4 to 5 minutes, or until soup is hot, stirring once.

Per Serving:

| | | | |
|---|---|---|---|
| Calories: | 227 | Fat: | 12 g. |
| Protein: | 14 g. | Sodium: | 866 mg. |
| Carbohydrate: | 19 g. | Cholesterol: | 51 mg. |

MENU

*Wild Rice Vegetable Soup*
*Hard Rolls\**
*Smoked*
*Cheddar Cheese Slices\**

## Time Management

- Cook wild rice conventionally.
- Microwave soup. • While soup microwaves, slice cheese.

# Wild Rice Vegetable Soup

½  cup thinly sliced carrots
½  cup thinly sliced celery
½  cup chopped onion
 1  tablespoon margarine or butter
 2  cans (14½ oz. each) ready-to-serve chicken broth
 1  to 1½ cups cut-up cooked chicken
 1  cup sliced fresh mushrooms
 1  cup cooked wild rice
¼  cup sherry
 1  teaspoon salt
½  teaspoon dried marjoram leaves
 1  cup torn fresh spinach leaves

4 to 6 servings

In 2-quart casserole, combine carrots, celery, onion and margarine. Cover. Microwave at High for 4 to 5 minutes, or until vegetables are tender-crisp, stirring once. Add chicken broth, chicken, mushrooms, cooked wild rice, sherry, salt and marjoram. Re-cover. Microwave at High for 6 to 8 minutes, or until soup is hot, stirring once. Add spinach. Microwave at High for 2 minutes, or until spinach is wilted.

Per Serving:
| | |
|---|---|
| Calories: | 145 |
| Protein: | 12 g. |
| Carbohydrate: | 11 g. |
| Fat: | 5 g. |
| Sodium: | 855 mg. |
| Cholesterol: | 21 mg. |

## Wild Mushroom Soup

| | |
|---|---|
| 1½ cups warm water | 1 can (12 oz.) evaporated milk |
| 3 dried morels (about 0.2 oz.) | 1 can (14½ oz.) ready-to-serve beef broth |
| ½ cup finely chopped carrot | |
| ¼ cup sliced green onions | 1 jar (7 oz.) sliced shiitake mushrooms, drained |
| ¼ cup margarine or butter | |
| ¼ cup plus 2 tablespoons all-purpose flour | 1 jar (4.5 oz.) whole mushrooms, drained |
| ½ teaspoon salt | ¼ cup brandy (optional) |
| ¼ teaspoon white pepper | |

4 to 6 servings

In 2-cup measure, combine water and morels. Set aside. In 2-quart casserole, combine carrot, onions and margarine. Cover. Microwave at High for 3 to 4 minutes, or until vegetables are tender. Stir in flour, salt and pepper. Blend in evaporated milk. Microwave, uncovered, at High for 4 to 6 minutes, or until mixture thickens and bubbles, stirring 3 or 4 times. Strain morels from water, reserving water. Chop morels. Add reserved water, chopped morels and remaining ingredients to thickened milk mixture. Cover. Microwave at High for 6 to 8 minutes, or until soup is hot, stirring once or twice. Garnish with snipped fresh parsley, if desired.

Per Serving:

| | | | |
|---|---|---|---|
| Calories: | 210 | Fat: | 13 g. |
| Protein: | 7 g. | Sodium: | 642 mg. |
| Carbohydrate: | 19 g. | Cholesterol: | 18 mg. |

# French Country-style Soup

½ cup coarsely chopped onion
1 medium carrot, thinly sliced
½ cup thinly sliced celery
2 tablespoons margarine or butter
1 tablespoon snipped fresh parsley
1 clove garlic, minced
½ teaspoon dried thyme leaves
1 bay leaf
1 can (16 oz.) baked beans
1 can (15 oz.) Great Northern beans, drained
1 can (14½ oz.) ready-to-serve chicken broth
1 cup water
2 fully cooked Polish sausages (2 oz. each), thinly sliced

4 to 6 servings

In 2-quart casserole, combine onion, carrot, celery, margarine, parsley, garlic, thyme and bay leaf. Cover. Microwave at High for 4 to 7 minutes, or until vegetables are tender, stirring once or twice. Add beans, chicken broth, water and sausage. Mix well. Re-cover. Microwave at High for 6 to 9 minutes, or until soup is hot, stirring once or twice. Remove bay leaf.

Per Serving:
Calories:         262
Protein:          13 g.
Carbohydrate:     27 g.
Fat:              12 g.
Sodium:           792 mg.
Cholesterol:      16 mg.

---

**MENU**

---

*Curry Shrimp Soup*        *Hot Herb Loaf*

---

**Time Management**

• Prepare herb butter. • Heat conventional oven while you start microwaving soup. • Slit and season bread; heat conventionally while soup microwaves.

## Curry Shrimp Soup ▶

| | |
|---|---|
| 1 cup frozen peas | ¼ teaspoon salt |
| ½ cup finely chopped carrot | ⅛ teaspoon white pepper |
| ⅓ cup chopped onion | 1 can (14½ oz.) ready-to-serve chicken broth |
| 2 tablespoons margarine or butter | ½ lb. medium shrimp, shelled and deveined |
| ¼ cup plus 2 tablespoons all-purpose flour | 2 cups half-and-half |
| 1½ teaspoons curry powder | ½ cup seeded chopped tomato (optional) |
| ½ teaspoon dried basil leaves | |

4 to 6 servings

In small mixing bowl, microwave peas at High for 2 to 2½ minutes, or until defrosted, stirring once. Set aside. In 2-quart casserole, combine carrot, onion and margarine. Cover. Microwave at High for 4 to 5½ minutes, or until vegetables are tender, stirring once. Stir in flour and seasonings. Blend in chicken broth. Microwave at High for 5 to 8 minutes, or until mixture thickens and bubbles, stirring after the first 2 minutes and then every minute. Add peas and shrimp. Blend in half-and-half. Microwave at 50% (Medium) for 13 to 18 minutes, or until shrimp are opaque, stirring 2 or 3 times. Stir in chopped tomato.

| Per Serving: | | | |
|---|---|---|---|
| Calories: | 236 | Fat: | 14 g. |
| Protein: | 12 g. | Sodium: | 457 mg. |
| Carbohydrate: | 15 g. | Cholesterol: | 73 mg. |

## Hot Herb Loaf ▶

1 loaf (1 lb.) French bread
¼ cup margarine or butter
½ cup shredded fresh Parmesan cheese
8 sprigs fresh basil

6 to 8 servings

Heat conventional oven to 400°F. Make 8 diagonal cuts in French bread just to within ½ inch of bottom crust. Set aside. In small bowl, microwave margarine at High for 1¼ to 1½ minutes, or until melted. Add cheese. Toss to coat with melted margarine. Spread margarine and cheese mixture evenly between bread slices. Insert fresh herb sprigs between bread slices. Wrap loaf in foil and secure ends. Heat 15 to 20 minutes, or until hot.

| Per Serving: | |
|---|---|
| Calories: | 245 |
| Protein: | 8 g. |
| Carbohydrate: | 32 g. |
| Fat: | 9 g. |
| Sodium: | 513 mg. |
| Cholesterol: | 7 mg. |

28

*Cracked Wheat Garden Salad*
*Fresh Fruit**

### Time Management

• The night before, or about 3 hours before serving, prepare bulgur. • Microwave zucchini and carrot. • Prepare lettuce; cover and refrigerate. • Mix dressing and combine with remaining salad ingredients. Chill 2 hours. • Just before serving, toss salad with lettuce.

## Cracked Wheat Garden Salad

**Salad:**
- 1 cup uncooked bulgur or cracked wheat
- 3 cups hot water
- ½ cup chopped carrot
- ½ cup chopped zucchini
- 1 lb. fully cooked ham, cut into 1 × ½-inch pieces
- 1 cup seeded chopped tomato
- ¼ cup coarsely chopped walnuts
- 4 cups torn leaf lettuce

**Dressing:**
- ⅓ cup olive or vegetable oil
- 2 tablespoons white vinegar
- 1 large clove garlic, minced
- ½ teaspoon salt
- ¼ teaspoon pepper

4 to 6 servings

Place bulgur in medium mixing bowl. Set aside. Place water in 4-cup measure. Cover with plastic wrap. Microwave at High for 5½ to 7 minutes, or until water boils. Pour boiling water over bulgur. Re-cover with plastic wrap. Let stand for 30 minutes. Drain bulgur, pressing out excess moisture. Set aside.

In medium mixing bowl, place carrot and zucchini. Cover with plastic wrap. Microwave at High for 2 to 3 minutes, or until carrot and zucchini are tender-crisp. Add bulgur and remaining salad ingredients, except leaf lettuce. In 1-cup measure, combine all dressing ingredients. Mix well. Pour dressing over salad. Toss to coat. Chill 2 hours. Before serving, add leaf lettuce. Toss to combine.

| Per Serving: | | | |
|---|---|---|---|
| Calories: | 360 | Fat: | 20 g. |
| Protein: | 20 g. | Sodium: | 1102 mg. |
| Carbohydrate: | 26 g. | Cholesterol: | 40 mg. |

## Southwest Spaghetti Salad

1 pkg. (7 oz.) uncooked spaghetti
1 tablespoon olive or vegetable oil
1 boneless whole chicken breast (8 to 10 oz.), skin removed, cut into 1-inch pieces
1 cup taco sauce, divided
1 can (16 oz.) pinto beans, drained
1 cup shredded Cheddar cheese
1 cup seeded chopped tomato
½ cup sliced black olives
¼ cup sliced green onions
  Leaf lettuce

4 to 6 servings

Prepare spaghetti as directed on package. Rinse and drain. Place cooked spaghetti in large mixing bowl or salad bowl. Sprinkle with oil. Toss to coat. Set aside.

In 1-quart casserole, combine chicken and ½ cup taco sauce. Cover. Microwave at High for 5 to 8 minutes, or until chicken is no longer pink, stirring once. Drain. Add cooked chicken, beans, cheese, tomato, olives and onions to cooked spaghetti. Toss gently to combine.

Line serving platter with leaf lettuce. Spoon salad onto serving platter. Spoon remaining ½ cup taco sauce over salad. Toss lightly before serving. Serve with additional taco sauce, if desired.

| Per Serving: | |
| --- | --- |
| Calories: | 379 |
| Protein: | 22 g. |
| Carbohydrate: | 42 g. |
| Fat: | 13 g. |
| Sodium: | 503 mg. |
| Cholesterol: | 44 mg. |

---

### *MENU*

*Southwest Spaghetti Salad*
*Tortilla Chips* *

---

### Time Management

• Cook spaghetti conventionally while you microwave chicken. • Assemble salad. • Serve with tortilla chips and additional taco sauce.

## Barbecued Turkey Salad

*MENU*

*Barbecued Turkey Salad*
*Bakery Rolls\**

**Time Management**

• Heat conventional oven and warm bakery rolls. • Microwave dressing. • Assemble salad. Add dressing just before serving.

**Dressing:**
¼ cup barbecue sauce
2 tablespoons vinegar
1 tablespoon catsup
1 teaspoon dry mustard
1 clove garlic, minced
¼ teaspoon salt
Dash cayenne
¼ cup vegetable oil

**Salad:**
1 lb. fresh spinach, trimmed and torn into bite-size pieces (about 8 cups)
1 cup cherry tomatoes, quartered
1 jar (7 oz.) whole baby corn, drained
½ cup thinly sliced red onion
¾ lb. barbecued turkey breast, cut into thin strips

4 to 6 servings

In small mixing bowl, combine all dressing ingredients except oil. Mix well. Cover with plastic wrap. Microwave at High for 1 to 2 minutes, or until mixture is hot. Gradually whisk in oil, until mixture is smooth. Set aside. On 12-inch platter, arrange spinach, tomatoes, baby corn, onion and turkey breast strips. Before serving, spoon dressing evenly over salad.

| Per Serving: | | | |
|---|---|---|---|
| Calories: | 214 | Fat: | 14 g. |
| Protein: | 16 g. | Sodium: | 977 mg. |
| Carbohydrate: | 9 g. | Cholesterol: | 47 mg. |

*MENU*

---

*Spanish Rice Salad*
*Easy Corn Muffins*

---

**Time Management**

• The night before, or early in the day, microwave rice mixture. • Chill at least 3 hours. • About 45 minutes before serving, heat conventional oven and prepare corn muffins. • While muffins bake, assemble salad.

## Spanish Rice Salad

1   pkg. (7½ oz.) rice and vermicelli mix with Spanish seasonings
2   tablespoons margarine or butter
2¼  cups hot water
1   can (16 oz.) whole tomatoes, cut up and undrained
1½  cups shredded Cheddar cheese
1   can (15½ oz.) dark red kidney beans, rinsed and drained
1   can (8 oz.) corn, drained
1   can (4 oz.) chopped green chilies, drained
3   tablespoons sliced green onions
¼   cup vegetable oil
2   tablespoons white vinegar

4 to 6 servings

Per Serving:
| | |
|---|---|
| Calories: | 452 |
| Protein: | 16 g. |
| Carbohydrate: | 46 g. |
| Fat: | 24 g. |
| Sodium: | 1550 mg. |
| Cholesterol: | 30 mg. |

## How to Microwave Spanish Rice Salad

**Combine** rice and vermicelli in 3-quart casserole. Add margarine. Microwave at High for 3 to 4 minutes, or until vermicelli is golden brown, stirring once.

**Add** water, tomatoes and seasoning packet. Cover. Microwave at High for 20 to 25 minutes, or until rice is tender and most of liquid is absorbed.

## Easy Corn Muffins

1 cup frozen corn
2 tablespoons margarine or
   butter
1 cup yellow cornmeal
1 cup all-purpose flour
2 tablespoons sugar
2 teaspoons baking powder
½ teaspoon salt
1 cup half-and-half
¼ cup vegetable oil
1 egg

1 dozen muffins

Heat conventional oven to 400°F. In 1-quart casserole, microwave corn at High for 2 to 2½ minutes, or until defrosted. Set aside. In small bowl, microwave margarine at High for 45 seconds to 1 minute, or until melted. Set aside. Line 12 muffin cups with paper liners. Set aside. In large mixing bowl, combine cornmeal, flour, sugar, baking powder and salt. Mix well. Add corn, melted margarine and remaining ingredients; stir just until dry ingredients are moistened. Spoon batter evenly into liners, filling two-thirds full. Bake for 20 to 25 minutes, or until golden brown. Remove muffins from pan and place on cooling rack.

Per Serving:
| | |
|---|---|
| Calories: | 185 |
| Protein: | 4 g. |
| Carbohydrate: | 21 g. |
| Fat: | 10 g. |
| Sodium: | 179 mg. |
| Cholesterol: | 30 mg. |

**Chill** salad at least 3 hours. Add cheese, kidney beans, corn, chilies and onions.

**Blend** oil and vinegar in 1-cup measure. Pour over salad. Toss to coat. Serve on bed of lettuce, if desired.

## MENU

*Teriyaki Tuna Salad*
*Refrigerated Crescent Rolls**

### Time Management

• Heat conventional oven and bake rolls as directed on package.
• While rolls bake, microwave tuna salad, toss with dressing and arrange on bed of lettuce. • Serve salad and rolls warm.

## Teriyaki Tuna Salad

### Dressing:

  2 tablespoons teriyaki sauce
  2 tablespoons vegetable oil
  2 tablespoons sliced green onion
  ¼ teaspoon ground ginger
  ¼ teaspoon sugar

### Salad:

  2 pkgs. (10 oz. each) frozen white and wild rice
  ⅓ cup shredded carrot
  2 cans (6½ oz. each) solid white tuna, water pack, drained and flaked
  1 can (8 oz.) sliced water chestnuts, drained
1½ cups fresh broccoli flowerets
  2 tablespoons water
    Leaf lettuce

4 to 6 servings

In 1-cup measure, blend all dressing ingredients. Set aside. Place rice in 2-quart casserole. Sprinkle with carrot. Cover. Microwave at High for 7 to 12 minutes, or until hot, stirring to break apart 2 or 3 times. Stir in tuna and water chestnuts. Re-cover. Set aside. In 1-quart casserole, combine broccoli and water. Cover. Microwave at High for 2 to 3 minutes, or until tender-crisp. Drain. Add to tuna mixture. Pour dressing over tuna salad. Toss lightly to coat. Serve warm on bed of lettuce.

| Per Serving: | |
| --- | --- |
| Calories: | 263 |
| Protein: | 21 g. |
| Carbohydrate: | 28 g. |
| Fat: | 7 g. |
| Sodium: | 687 mg. |
| Cholesterol: | 39 mg. |

## BLT & Avocado Salad

**Salad:**

- 8 slices bacon
- 8 cups torn leaf lettuce
- 1 avocado, peeled and cut into 12 wedges
- 1 large tomato, cut into 12 wedges
- 1 cup seasoned croutons

**Dressing:**

- ¼ cup sour cream
- ¼ cup mayonnaise
- ¼ cup buttermilk
- ½ teaspoon dried parsley flakes
- ⅛ teaspoon salt
- ⅛ teaspoon pepper

4 to 6 servings

Layer 3 paper towels on plate. Arrange bacon on paper towels. Cover with another paper towel. Microwave at High for 7 to 10 minutes, or until bacon is brown and crisp, rotating twice. Set aside. In large mixing bowl or salad bowl, combine lettuce, avocado wedges, tomato wedges and croutons. Cut cooked bacon slices into 1½-inch lengths. Add to lettuce mixture. In small mixing bowl, blend all dressing ingredients. Pour over salad. Toss to coat.

Per Serving:
| | |
|---|---|
| Calories: | 254 |
| Protein: | 6 g. |
| Carbohydrate: | 11 g. |
| Fat: | 21 g. |
| Sodium: | 377 mg. |
| Cholesterol: | 19 mg. |

**Time Management**

• Prepare all ingredients. • Microwave beef rolls to melt cheese. • Assemble sandwiches.

## Hot Cheese-stuffed Roast Beef Sandwiches

4 French rolls (6 to 8-inch)
   Horseradish sauce
½ cup shredded Cheddar cheese
½ lb. fully cooked roast beef, thinly sliced (8 slices)
8 tomato slices
8 small whole green onions
8 lettuce leaves

4 servings

Split French rolls lengthwise. Spread each half with horseradish sauce. Arrange bottom halves of rolls on paper-towel-lined plate. Set aside. Set top halves of rolls aside. Sprinkle 1 tablespoon of cheese down the center of each beef slice. Roll up. Cut each roll-up in half crosswise. Arrange 4 halves on each bottom half of French rolls. Microwave at 70% (Medium High) for 2 to 3½ minutes, or until cheese melts, rotating plate once. Top each roll with 2 tomato slices, 2 green onions and 2 lettuce leaves. Top each sandwich with top halves of rolls.

| Per Serving: | |
| --- | --- |
| Calories: | 313 |
| Protein: | 22 g. |
| Carbohydrate: | 24 g. |
| Fat: | 14 g. |
| Sodium: | 349 mg. |
| Cholesterol: | 63 mg. |

## MENU

*Olive & Salami
Sandwich Loaf*
*Fresh Fruit\**

### Time Management

• The night before, or about 2½ hours before serving, hollow out loaf and microwave filling. • Assemble sandwich loaf; wrap and chill at least 2 hours. • Prepare fruit; cover and refrigerate until serving time.

## Olive & Salami Sandwich Loaf

| | |
|---|---|
| 1 loaf (1 lb.) French bread | 2 tablespoons white vinegar |
| 4 oz. cream cheese | 1 clove garlic, minced |
| ½ teaspoon Italian seasoning | ½ cup chopped black olives |
| ½ cup chopped green pepper | ½ cup chopped pimiento- |
| ½ cup chopped red pepper | stuffed green olives |
| ¼ cup chopped onion | ¼ lb. salami, thinly sliced |
| ⅓ cup olive or vegetable oil | |

6 to 8 servings

Slice French bread in half lengthwise. Remove bread from center of loaf halves to within ½ inch of crust. Reserve bread for future use. Set loaf halves aside. In small bowl, microwave cream cheese at High for 30 to 45 seconds, or until softened. Add Italian seasoning. Mix well. Spread cream cheese mixture evenly over inside top and bottom of loaf. Set aside.

In 1-quart casserole, combine the green and red pepper, onion, oil, vinegar and garlic. Mix well. Cover. Microwave at High for 3 to 4 minutes, or until vegetables are tender-crisp, stirring once. Add olives. Mix well. Spoon vegetable mixture evenly over inside top and bottom of loaf. Arrange salami evenly over bottom half of loaf. Place top of loaf over salami. Wrap in plastic wrap and chill at least 2 hours or overnight. Slice diagonally into serving-size pieces.

| Per Serving: | | | |
|---|---|---|---|
| Calories: | 359 | Fat: | 21 g. |
| Protein: | 9 g. | Sodium: | 808 mg. |
| Carbohydrate: | 34 g. | Cholesterol: | 26 mg. |

MENU

*Chili Chicken Croissants*
*Pickled Peppers**

**Time Management**

• The night before, or 2½ hours before serving, microwave chicken and prepare filling. Chill at least 2 hours. • Assemble sandwiches and serve with pickled peppers.

# Chili Chicken Croissants

   1 lb. boneless whole chicken
      breast, skin removed, cut
      into ¾-inch pieces
   ½ teaspoon chili powder
   ¼ teaspoon salt
   1 small clove garlic, minced
   ¼ cup sliced celery
   ¼ cup sliced green onions
   ¼ cup chopped red pepper
   2 tablespoons mayonnaise
   2 tablespoons sour cream
   1 tablespoon canned chopped
      green chilies
   4 croissants, split
      Leaf lettuce

4 servings

In 2-quart casserole, combine chicken, chili powder, salt and garlic. Cover. Microwave at High for 4 to 6 minutes, or until chicken is no longer pink, stirring twice. Drain. Add celery, onions, red pepper, mayonnaise, sour cream and chilies. Mix well. Chill at least 2 hours. To serve, line each croissant with leaf lettuce and divide chicken mixture into fourths. Spoon one-fourth of mixture into each croissant.

| Per Serving: | |
| --- | --- |
| Calories: | 390 |
| Protein: | 31 g. |
| Carbohydrate: | 22 g. |
| Fat: | 19 g. |
| Sodium: | 413 mg. |
| Cholesterol: | 80 mg. |

## Curried Shrimp-stuffed Pitas

### MENU

*Curried Shrimp-stuffed Pitas*
*Apple Wedges\**

#### Time Management

• Microwave curried shrimp filling.
• Cut apple wedges. • Assemble and heat pitas.

1 small zucchini, cut in half
  lengthwise and thinly sliced
¼ cup chopped red pepper
2 tablespoons chopped onion
1 pkg. (6 oz.) frozen cooked
  small shrimp, defrosted

⅓ cup chopped marinated
  artichoke hearts
2 tablespoons sour cream
2 tablespoons mayonnaise
¼ teaspoon curry powder
4 lettuce leaves
2 pitas (6-inch), cut in half

4 servings

In 1-quart casserole, place zucchini, red pepper and onion. Cover. Microwave at High for 1 to 2 minutes, or until vegetables are tender-crisp. Stir in shrimp, artichoke hearts, sour cream, mayonnaise and curry powder. Mix well. Set aside. Place lettuce leaf in each pita half. Spoon shrimp mixture evenly into pita halves. Place on paper-towel-lined plate. Microwave at High for 1 to 2 minutes, or until pitas feel warm to the touch.

Per Serving:
Calories: 177    Fat: 9 g.
Protein: 12 g.    Sodium: 165 mg.
Carbohydrate: 12 g.    Cholesterol: 90 mg.

## MENU

*Salmon-Vegetable Spread on Rye*
*Honeydew Melon or Grapes**

### Time Management

• The night before, or early in the day, hard-cook eggs conventionally and microwave spread. Cover and refrigerate at least 2 hours.
• Prepare fruit. • Assemble and garnish open-face sandwiches.

## Salmon-Vegetable Spread on Rye

½  cup finely chopped carrot
½  cup finely chopped celery
½  cup finely chopped onion
2  cans (6¾ oz. each) skinless, boneless salmon, drained
1  pkg. (3 oz.) cream cheese
¼  cup mayonnaise

1  tablespoon snipped fresh dill weed or ½ teaspoon dried dill weed
½  teaspoon salt
6  slices rye bread
3  hard-cooked eggs, sliced
12  thin cucumber slices

6 servings

In 1-quart casserole, combine carrot, celery and onion. Cover. Microwave at High for 2 to 3 minutes, or until vegetables are tender-crisp. Add salmon to vegetable mixture. Set aside. In small mixing bowl, microwave cream cheese at High for 15 to 30 seconds, or until softened. Add mayonnaise, dill weed and salt. Mix well. Add to vegetable-salmon mixture. Mix well. Cover and chill mixture 2 hours. To serve, spread each slice of bread evenly with salmon and vegetable mixture. Top each open-face sandwich with 2 hard-cooked egg slices and 2 cucumber slices. Garnish with sprigs of fresh dill, if desired.

Per Serving:
| | | | |
|---|---|---|---|
| Calories: | 337 | Fat: | 22 g. |
| Protein: | 18 g. | Sodium: | 499 mg. |
| Carbohydrate: | 17 g. | Cholesterol: | 178 mg. |

43

| *Oven-fried Fish* | *Basiled New Potatoes* | *Marinated Summer Vegetables* |

## Time Management

• The night before, or at least 3 hours before serving, microwave marinated vegetables. • About ½ hour before serving, heat conventional oven while you prepare fish and potatoes for cooking. • Microwave potatoes and bake fish conventionally.

## Oven-fried Fish

| ¼ | cup vegetable oil, divided | 1 | can (5 oz.) evaporated milk |
| 4 | cups crisp rice cereal | 1 | egg |
| 1½ | teaspoons paprika | 1¼ | lbs. sole fillets, about ⅛ to ¼ |
| ½ | teaspoon salt | | inch thick, cut into serving- |
| ½ | teaspoon pepper | | size pieces |

4 to 6 servings

Heat conventional oven to 425°F. Drizzle 2 tablespoons of the oil in a 15½ × 10½-inch shallow baking pan. Set aside. Place cereal in food processor or blender. Process until fine. Mix cereal crumbs, paprika, salt and pepper on a sheet of wax paper. In 9-inch pie plate, blend milk and egg. Dip fillets into egg mixture, then into crumb mixture, pressing lightly to coat both sides. Arrange fillets in single layer in prepared baking pan. Drizzle tops of fillets with remaining 2 tablespoons of oil. Bake for 8 to 10 minutes, or until fish flakes easily with fork.

Per Serving:
| Calories: | 309 | Fat: | 14 g. |
| Protein: | 25 g. | Sodium: | 535 mg. |
| Carbohydrate: | 19 g. | Cholesterol: | 108 mg. |

## Basiled New Potatoes

| 1 | lb. new potatoes (about 8) | 1 | teaspoon dried basil leaves |
| ¼ | cup water | ⅛ | teaspoon garlic salt |
| 2 | tablespoons margarine or | | Dash pepper |
| | butter | | |

4 to 6 servings

Remove thin strip of peel from center of each potato. Place potatoes in 1½-quart casserole. Add water. Cover. Microwave at High for 7 to 9 minutes, or until potatoes are tender, stirring once. Let stand, covered, for 5 minutes. Drain. Place remaining ingredients in 1-cup measure. Microwave at High for 45 seconds to 1 minute, or until margarine is melted. Stir. Pour over potatoes. Toss to coat.

Per Serving:
| Calories: | 101 | Fat: | 4 g. |
| Protein: | 1 g. | Sodium: | 54 mg. |
| Carbohydrate: | 15 g. | Cholesterol: | — |

## ◄ Marinated Summer Vegetables

| 1 | pkg. (9 oz.) frozen small |
| | whole green beans |
| 1 | small onion, thinly sliced and |
| | separated into rings |
| 2 | tablespoons water |
| 1 | small yellow squash, cut into |
| | thin diagonal slices |
| ¼ | cup chopped red pepper or |
| | 1 jar (2 oz.) sliced pimiento, |
| | drained |
| ½ | cup Italian dressing |

4 to 6 servings

In 1½-quart casserole, place beans and onion. Add water. Cover. Microwave at High for 6 to 8 minutes, or until beans are tender-crisp, stirring once. Add squash and red pepper. Re-cover. Microwave at High for 1 to 2 minutes, or until squash is tender-crisp. Drain. Add dressing. Toss to coat. Re-cover. Chill at least 2 hours, or overnight. Drain before serving.

Per Serving:
| Calories: | 41 |
| Protein: | 1 g. |
| Carbohydrate: | 4 g. |
| Fat: | 3 g. |
| Sodium: | 45 mg. |
| Cholesterol: | — |

## MENU

*Tuna Noodle Parmesan*
*Carrot & Celery Sticks, Olives\**

### Time Management

• Boil water for noodles while you prepare and chill carrots and celery. • Microwave tuna sauce while noodles cook conventionally.

## Tuna Noodle Parmesan

- 1  pkg. (10 oz.) uncooked wide egg noodles
- 1  tablespoon olive oil
- 1  pkg. (10 oz.) frozen peas
- 1  pkg. (1.75 oz.) white sauce mix
- ¼  teaspoon instant minced garlic
- ¼  teaspoon fennel seed, crushed
     Dash pepper
- 1¾  cups milk
- 1  can (9¼ oz.) tuna, water pack, drained and flaked
- 1  medium tomato, seeded and chopped
- ¼  cup shredded fresh Parmesan cheese

4 to 6 servings

Prepare egg noodles as directed on package. Rinse and drain. Toss with olive oil. Cover to keep warm. Set aside. Place peas in 1-quart casserole. Cover. Microwave at High for 3 to 5 minutes, or until defrosted, stirring once to break apart. Drain. Set aside.

In 1½-quart casserole, place white sauce mix, garlic, fennel and pepper. Blend in milk. Microwave at High for 7 to 9 minutes; or until mixture thickens and bubbles, stirring 2 or 3 times. Add peas and tuna to sauce. Mix well. Cover. Microwave at High for 3 to 4 minutes, or until peas are hot, stirring once. Arrange cooked noodles in even layer on large serving platter. Spoon tuna mixture over noodles. Top with tomatoes. Sprinkle with cheese.

| Per Serving: | | | |
|---|---|---|---|
| Calories: | 389 | Fat: | 10 g. |
| Protein: | 26 g. | Sodium: | 462 mg. |
| Carbohydrate: | 49 g. | Cholesterol: | 81 mg. |

### Time Management

• Cut vegetable ribbons; combine with margarine and seasonings.
• Prepare fish fillets and broil conventionally. • When fillets have cooked 4 to 5 minutes, microwave vegetables.

## Lemon Thyme Fish Fillets

1   tablespoon plus 1½ teaspoons margarine or butter
½   teaspoon dried thyme leaves
¼   teaspoon onion salt
4   drops red pepper sauce
1¼  lbs. orange roughy fillets, about ½ to ¾ inch thick, cut into serving-size pieces
6   thin lemon slices
    Fresh parsley sprigs (optional)

4 to 6 servings

In small bowl, combine margarine, thyme, onion salt and red pepper sauce. Microwave at High for 45 seconds to 1 minute, or until margarine is melted. Set aside. Arrange fillets on conventional broiler pan. Brush evenly with margarine mixture. Top with lemon slices. Place fish under conventional broiler, 4 to 5 inches from heat. Broil about 8 to 10 minutes, or until fish flakes easily with fork. Garnish each fillet with parsley sprig.

Per Serving:
| | |
|---|---|
| Calories: | 258 |
| Protein: | 25 g. |
| Carbohydrate: | 2 g. |
| Fat: | 16 g. |
| Sodium: | 259 mg. |
| Cholesterol: | 34 mg. |

## Carrot & Squash Ribbons ▲

2   medium carrots
1   small zucchini (about 4 oz.)
1   small summer squash (about 4 oz.)
2   tablespoons margarine or butter, cut up
    Dash garlic powder

4 to 6 servings

Using vegetable peeler, cut lengthwise ribbons from each vegetable, discarding center portion of vegetables. In 1½-quart casserole, combine vegetable ribbons. Top with margarine. Sprinkle with garlic powder. Cover. Microwave at High for 3 to 4 minutes, or until vegetables are tender-crisp. Toss to coat with margarine.

Per Serving:
| | | | |
|---|---|---|---|
| Calories: | 51 | Fat: | 4 g. |
| Protein: | 1 g. | Sodium: | 54 mg. |
| Carbohydrate: | 4 g. | Cholesterol: | — |

## MENU

*Creole Quiche*
*Spinach-Apple Salad*

### Time Management

• Heat conventional oven and prepare pie crust. • While crust bakes, microwave filling. Assemble quiche. • While quiche bakes conventionally, prepare ingredients for salad. • Five minutes before serving, microwave dressing and toss salad.

## Creole Quiche ▲

- 1 pkg. (15 oz.) refrigerated prepared pie crusts
- ¼ cup finely chopped green pepper
- ¼ cup chopped onion
- 2 tablespoons margarine or butter
- 2 tablespoons all-purpose flour
- ¼ to ½ teaspoon cayenne
- ¼ teaspoon salt
- ⅛ teaspoon pepper
- 4 eggs, beaten
- ½ cup milk
- 1 can (4½ oz.) small shrimp, rinsed and drained
- ¾ cup seeded chopped tomato
- ½ cup shredded Cheddar cheese

4 to 6 servings

Heat conventional oven to 450°F. Let one pie crust stand at room temperature for 15 to 20 minutes. Return remaining pie crust to refrigerator for future use. Unfold crust, ease into 9-inch pie plate and flute edge. Bake for 8 to 10 minutes, or until lightly browned. Set aside.

Reduce oven temperature to 350°F. In 1½-quart casserole, combine green pepper, onion and margarine. Cover. Microwave at High for 2 to 3 minutes, or until vegetables are tender-crisp. Stir in flour, cayenne, salt and pepper. Blend in eggs, milk, shrimp, tomato and cheese. Microwave at High for 3 to 5 minutes, or until mixture is hot and begins to set around edges, stirring with whisk after every minute. Pour into prepared crust. Bake for 18 to 22 minutes, or until center of filling is set. Let stand for 10 minutes.

| Per Serving: | | | |
|---|---|---|---|
| Calories: | 333 | Fat: | 21 g. |
| Protein: | 13 g. | Sodium: | 418 mg. |
| Carbohydrate: | 21 g. | Cholesterol: | 223 mg. |

## Spinach-Apple Salad ▲

1 lb. fresh spinach, trimmed
   and torn into bite-size
   pieces (about 8 cups)
1 small apple, cored and cut
   into thin wedges
¼ cup sliced green onions
1 tablespoon lemon juice
4 slices bacon, cut into ½-inch
   pieces
¼ cup vinegar
¼ cup water
2 tablespoons sugar
1 tablespoon brandy (optional)

4 to 6 servings

Place spinach in large mixing bowl or salad bowl. In small mixing bowl, combine apple and onions. Sprinkle with lemon juice. Add to spinach. Toss to combine. Set aside. Place bacon pieces in 1-quart casserole. Cover with paper towel. Microwave at High for 4½ to 7 minutes, or until bacon is brown and crisp, stirring once to break apart. Remove bacon pieces from drippings and drain on paper towel. Set aside.

Add vinegar, water, sugar and brandy to bacon drippings in casserole. Microwave at High for 1½ to 2 minutes, or just until mixture begins to boil. Pour hot dressing over spinach mixture. Add bacon pieces. Toss to combine.

| Per Serving: | | | |
|---|---|---|---|
| Calories: | 77 | Fat: | 3 g. |
| Protein: | 4 g. | Sodium: | 140 mg. |
| Carbohydrate: | 11 g. | Cholesterol: | 4 mg. |

| *Creamed Salmon Dijon* | *Herbed Popovers* | *Gingered Orange-glazed Carrots* |

## Time Management

• Heat conventional oven and prepare popovers. • While popovers bake, microwave salmon mixture. • Set salmon aside while microwaving carrots. If needed, microwave salmon at High for 1 to 2 minutes, or until hot.

## Creamed Salmon Dijon

1 pkg. (10 oz.) frozen tiny peas
2 tablespoons finely chopped onion
1 tablespoon margarine or butter
2 cups milk
1 pkg. (1.75 oz.) white sauce mix
1 teaspoon Dijon mustard
¼ teaspoon dried thyme leaves
1 egg yolk
2 cans (6¾ oz. each) skinless, boneless salmon, drained

4 to 6 servings

Place peas in 1-quart casserole. Cover. Microwave at High for 3 to 5 minutes, or until defrosted, stirring once to break apart. Drain. Set aside.

In 1½-quart casserole, combine onion and margarine. Microwave at High for 1 to 1½ minutes, or until margarine is melted. Add milk, white sauce mix, mustard and thyme. Blend with whisk. Microwave at High for 5 to 11 minutes, or until sauce thickens and bubbles, stirring with whisk 3 or 4 times. Stir small amount of hot mixture into egg yolk. Blend egg yolk back into hot mixture. Stir in peas and salmon. Cover. Microwave at High for 2 to 2½ minutes, or until mixture is hot. Serve over Herbed Popovers (right).

Per Serving:
Calories: 240
Protein: 17 g.
Carbohydrate: 15 g.
Fat: 12 g.
Sodium: 448 mg.
Cholesterol: 69 mg.

## Herbed Popovers

1 cup all-purpose flour
1 tablespoon grated Parmesan cheese
1 teaspoon sugar
1 teaspoon dried parsley flakes
½ teaspoon seasoned salt
¼ teaspoon dried thyme leaves
1 cup milk
3 eggs

6 popovers

Heat conventional oven to 425°F. Generously grease 6-cup popover pan with shortening. Set aside. In medium mixing bowl, combine flour, Parmesan cheese, sugar, parsley, salt and thyme. Mix well. Add milk. Beat on medium speed of electric mixer for 30 seconds. Add eggs, one at a time, beating well after each addition. Fill popover cups one-half full with batter. Bake for 20 minutes. Reduce oven temperature to 325°F and bake for 15 to 20 minutes longer, or until popovers are deep golden brown. Remove from pan immediately. Serve hot.

Per Serving:
Calories: 148
Protein: 7 g.
Carbohydrate: 19 g.
Fat: 4 g.
Sodium: 226 mg.
Cholesterol: 142 mg.

## ◄ Gingered Orange-glazed Carrots

2 cups thinly sliced carrots
2 tablespoons water
2 tablespoons packed dark brown sugar
2 tablespoons orange marmalade
1 teaspoon margarine or butter
¼ teaspoon ground ginger
⅛ teaspoon salt

4 to 6 servings

In 1-quart casserole, combine carrots and water. Cover. Microwave at High for 4 to 7 minutes, or until carrots are tender, stirring once. Drain. Set aside. In 2-cup measure, place remaining ingredients. Microwave at High for 1 to 1½ minutes, or until mixture boils. Stir. Microwave for 1 minute. Pour over carrots. Toss to coat.

Per Serving:
Calories: 58
Protein: —
Carbohydrate: 13 g.
Fat: 1 g.
Sodium: 69 mg.
Cholesterol: —

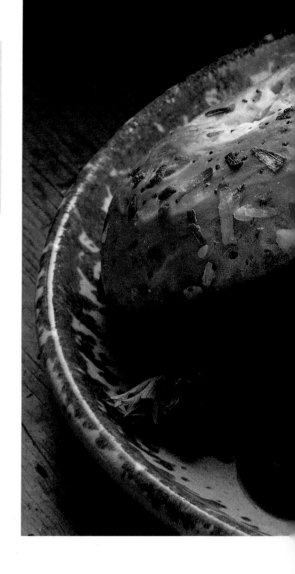

### Time Management

• Prepare carrot and celery sticks; cover and chill. • Prepare honey butter. Cover and set aside. • Mix and shape burgers. • Broil burgers conventionally while you microwave corn. • While corn stands, microwave gravy.

## Saucy Mushroom-stuffed Burgers ▶

| | |
|---|---|
| 1½ lbs. ground beef | 1½ cups chopped fresh mushrooms |
| ⅔ cup seasoned croutons, finely crushed | ¼ teaspoon salt |
| 1 egg | 1½ cups sliced fresh mushrooms |
| 3 tablespoons chopped onion | 2 tablespoons margarine or butter |
| 3 tablespoons snipped fresh parsley, divided | 1 pkg. (0.75 oz.) mushroom gravy mix |
| 1 tablespoon Dijon mustard | ¾ cup water |
| ¼ teaspoon pepper | 4 onion bagels |
| ¼ teaspoon salt | |
| 3 oz. cream cheese | |

4 servings

Per Serving:

| | | | |
|---|---|---|---|
| Calories: | 722 | Fat: | 42 g. |
| Protein: | 41 g. | Sodium: | 1236 mg. |
| Carbohydrate: | 42 g. | Cholesterol: | 206 mg. |

## How to Make Saucy Mushroom-stuffed Burgers

**Combine** ground beef, croutons, egg, onion, 2 tablespoons parsley, the mustard, pepper and salt in medium mixing bowl. Shape ground beef mixture into 8 patties, each about 4 inches in diameter. Set aside.

**Microwave** cream cheese in 1-quart casserole at High for 15 to 30 seconds, or until softened. Add chopped mushrooms, remaining 1 tablespoon parsley and the salt. Mix well.

**Mound** ¼ cup cream cheese mixture in center of each of 4 patties. Top with remaining patties. Pinch edges to seal securely. Place burgers on conventional broiler pan. Place under conventional broiler 3 inches from heat. Broil until medium doneness, about 5 to 7 minutes on each side.

## Honey-buttered Corn ▲

½ cup margarine or butter
1 tablespoon honey
1 tablespoon snipped fresh
   parsley

4 ears corn on the cob, husks
   removed

4 servings

In small mixing bowl, microwave margarine at 30% (Medium Low) for 15 seconds to 1 minute, or until softened, checking every 15 seconds. Stir in honey and parsley. Set aside. Rinse corn with water. Wrap each ear in plastic wrap. Arrange ears in single layer in microwave oven. Microwave at High for 8 to 16 minutes, or until corn is tender and brightens in color, rearranging ears once. Let stand 5 minutes. Serve honey butter with hot cooked corn.

| Per Serving: | | | |
|---|---|---|---|
| Calories: | 287 | Fat: | 24 g. |
| Protein: | 3 g. | Sodium: | 281 mg. |
| Carbohydrate: | 19 g. | Cholesterol: | — |

**Place** sliced mushrooms and margarine in 1-quart casserole. Microwave at High for 2 to 3 minutes, or until margarine is melted. Add gravy mix. Mix well. Blend in water. Microwave at High for 8 to 10 minutes, or until mixture thickens and bubbles, stirring 2 or 3 times. Serve burgers on bagels with gravy.

| *Spicy Italian Meatballs* | *Spaghetti Primavera* | *Tomato, Provolone & Red Onion Salad* |

### Time Management

• 1¼ hours before serving, prepare and chill salad. • About 25 minutes before serving, heat water conventionally while you shape meatballs. • Microwave meatballs and cut up vegetables for primavera while spaghetti boils. • Microwave vegetables while meatballs stand. • Toss vegetables with spaghetti and serve as a side dish.

## ◄ Spicy Italian Meatballs

| 1 | can (8 oz.) tomato sauce | ¾ | teaspoon Italian seasoning |
|---|---|---|---|
| ¼ | teaspoon sugar | ½ | teaspoon crushed red |
| ½ | lb. lean ground beef | | pepper flakes |
| ½ | lb. ground pork | ¼ | teaspoon salt |
| 1 | egg | 1 | tablespoon snipped fresh |
| 3 | tablespoons unseasoned dry | | parsley (optional) |
| | bread crumbs | | |

4 to 6 servings

In 2-quart casserole, blend tomato sauce and sugar. Set aside. In medium mixing bowl, combine remaining ingredients, except parsley. Mix well. Shape into 12 meatballs, about 1¾ inches in diameter. Add meatballs to sauce. Cover with wax paper. Microwave at High for 8 to 11 minutes, or until meatballs are firm and no longer pink, stirring once or twice to rearrange. Let stand, covered, for 5 minutes. Before serving, sprinkle with parsley.

| Per Serving: | | | |
|---|---|---|---|
| Calories: | 159 | Fat: | 7 g. |
| Protein: | 19 g. | Sodium: | 388 mg. |
| Carbohydrate: | 4 g. | Cholesterol: | 100 mg. |

## ◄ Spaghetti Primavera

| 1 | pkg. (7 oz.) uncooked | 1 | clove garlic, minced |
|---|---|---|---|
| | spaghetti | 2 | tablespoons olive oil |
| 1 | small summer squash (about | 3 | tablespoons grated Parmesan |
| | 4 oz.), cut in half lengthwise | | cheese |
| | and thinly sliced | | |
| 1 | small zucchini (about 4 oz.), | | |
| | cut in half lengthwise and | | |
| | thinly sliced | | |

4 to 6 servings

Prepare spaghetti as directed on package. Rinse and drain. Set aside. In 2-quart casserole, combine squash, zucchini, garlic and oil. Cover. Microwave at High for 3 to 4 minutes, or until vegetables are tender-crisp, stirring once. Add spaghetti and Parmesan cheese. Toss to coat.

| Per Serving: | | | |
|---|---|---|---|
| Calories: | 183 | Fat: | 6 g. |
| Protein: | 6 g. | Sodium: | 60 mg. |
| Carbohydrate: | 26 g. | Cholesterol: | 2 mg. |

## ◄ Tomato, Provolone & Red Onion Salad

| 2 | large tomatoes, sliced |
|---|---|
| | (¼-inch slices) |
| 3 | slices (1 oz. each) Provolone |
| | cheese, cut into halves |
| ⅓ | cup coarsely chopped red |
| | onion |
| 1 | tablespoon snipped fresh |
| | parsley |
| 8 | small whole fresh basil leaves |
| | or ½ teaspoon dried basil |
| | leaves |
| 2 | tablespoons olive oil |
| 2 | teaspoons red wine vinegar |
| ½ | teaspoon salt |
| ⅛ | teaspoon pepper |

4 to 6 servings

Arrange tomato slices in 12 × 8-inch baking dish or shallow serving dish. Top with cheese, onion, parsley and basil. Set aside. In 1-cup measure, blend remaining ingredients. Pour evenly over tomato mixture. Cover with plastic wrap. Chill at least 1 hour before serving.

| Per Serving: | |
|---|---|
| Calories: | 102 |
| Protein: | 4 g. |
| Carbohydrate: | 3 g. |
| Fat: | 8 g. |
| Sodium: | 309 mg. |
| Cholesterol: | 10 mg. |

*Sirloin & Fresh Vegetable Stroganoff*
*French Bread with Herb Butter\**

### Time Management

• Broil steak and heat water while you cut up vegetables. • Microwave vegetables; boil noodles conventionally. • Microwave sauce; spread noodles on plate; slice meat. • Reheat meat and vegetables in sauce; serve over noodles.

## Sirloin & Fresh Vegetable Stroganoff

1-lb. boneless beef sirloin steak, about 1 inch thick
2 teaspoons coarsely ground pepper
1 pkg. (10 oz.) uncooked wide egg noodles
1 tablespoon margarine or butter, cut up (optional)
2 cups fresh broccoli flowerets
1 cup julienne carrots (2 × ¼-inch strips)

1 cup frozen small whole onions
2 tablespoons water
1 pkg. (0.87 oz.) brown gravy mix
1 cup cold water
1 tablespoon catsup
1 teaspoon Worcestershire sauce
⅓ cup sour cream

4 to 6 servings

| Per Serving: | | | |
|---|---|---|---|
| Calories: | 375 | Fat: | 11 g. |
| Protein: | 25 g. | Sodium: | 304 mg. |
| Carbohydrate: | 44 g. | Cholesterol: | 94 mg. |

## How to Make Sirloin & Fresh Vegetable Stroganoff

**Sprinkle** each side of steak evenly with pepper. Press pepper lightly to adhere to surface of meat.

**Place** meat on conventional broiler pan. Place meat under conventional broiler, 4 inches from heat. Broil 5 to 7 minutes on each side, or until desired doneness. Let meat stand for 5 minutes. Slice thinly. Set aside.

**Prepare** egg noodles as directed on package. Rinse and drain. Arrange cooked egg noodles in an even layer on serving platter. Dot with margarine. Cover to keep warm. Set aside.

**Combine** broccoli, carrots, onions and water in 2-quart casserole. Cover. Microwave at High for 6 to 8 minutes, or until vegetables are tender, stirring once. Drain. Set aside.

**Place** brown gravy mix in 4-cup measure. Add water. Stir with whisk to combine. Microwave at High for 3 to 5 minutes, or until mixture thickens and bubbles, stirring with whisk after the first 2 minutes and then every minute.

**Add** catsup, Worcestershire sauce and sour cream. Stir with whisk until smooth. Add meat and sauce to vegetable mixture. Stir to combine. Cover. Microwave at High for 1 to 2 minutes, or until hot. Spoon over cooked egg noodles.

| *Mexican Stir-fry* | *Gazpacho Rice* | *Cheese & Pepper Corn Bread* |

**Time Management**

• Heat conventional oven and prepare corn bread. • While bread bakes, microwave rice. Prepare remaining ingredients for rice and the stir-fry. • Sauté stir-fry conventionally. • Garnish rice before serving.

## Mexican Stir-fry

1 -lb. boneless beef sirloin
   steak, about ¾ inch thick,
   cut into thin strips
½ teaspoon chili powder
½ teaspoon salt
¼ teaspoon ground cumin
¼ teaspoon garlic powder
2 tablespoons vegetable oil,
   divided

1 medium summer squash,
   thinly sliced
1 medium zucchini, thinly sliced
1 small red bell pepper, cut into
   julienne strips (2 × ¼-inch)
1 medium red onion, thinly
   sliced

4 servings

In large plastic food-storage bag, combine steak and seasonings. Shake to coat. Set aside. In deep 10-inch skillet, heat 1 tablespoon oil conventionally over medium-high heat until hot. Add squash, zucchini and pepper. Stir-fry for 2 to 4 minutes, or until vegetables are tender-crisp. Remove vegetables from skillet. Place vegetables in 2-quart casserole. Cover to keep warm. Set aside. Add remaining 1 tablespoon oil to skillet. Heat oil until hot. Add seasoned steak strips and onion. Stir-fry for about 5 minutes, or until meat is no longer pink. Using slotted spoon, remove meat and onion from skillet and add to vegetable mixture. Toss to combine.

Per Serving:

| | | | |
|---|---|---|---|
| Calories: | 261 | Fat: | 15 g. |
| Protein: | 26 g. | Sodium: | 295 mg. |
| Carbohydrate: | 5 g. | Cholesterol: | 65 mg. |

## Gazpacho Rice

1 cup uncooked long-grain
   white rice
1 cup tomato juice
1 cup hot water

1 teaspoon instant chicken
   bouillon granules
½ cup seeded chopped
   cucumber
½ cup seeded chopped tomato

4 to 6 servings

In 2-quart casserole, combine rice, tomato juice, water and bouillon. Cover. Microwave at High for 5 minutes. Microwave at 50% (Medium) for 12 to 15 minutes longer, or until rice is tender and liquid is absorbed. Let stand, covered, for 5 minutes. Add cucumber and tomato to rice mixture. Stir to combine.

Per Serving:

| | | | |
|---|---|---|---|
| Calories: | 124 | Fat: | — |
| Protein: | 3 g. | Sodium: | 211 mg. |
| Carbohydrate: | 27 g. | Cholesterol: | — |

## ◀ Cheese & Pepper Corn Bread

1 cup frozen corn
2 tablespoons margarine or
   butter
1 cup yellow cornmeal
1 cup all-purpose flour
2 tablespoons sugar
2 teaspoons baking powder
½ teaspoon salt
½ cup shredded Cheddar
   cheese
¼ cup chopped green pepper
2 tablespoons chopped onion
¼ to ½ teaspoon crushed red
   pepper flakes
1 cup half-and-half
¼ cup vegetable oil
1 egg

9 servings

Heat conventional oven to 400°F. Grease 9-inch square baking pan. Set aside. In 1-quart casserole, microwave corn at High for 2 to 2½ minutes, or until defrosted. Set aside. In small bowl, microwave margarine at High for 45 seconds to 1 minute, or until melted. Set aside. In large mixing bowl, combine cornmeal, flour, sugar, baking powder and salt. Mix well. Add corn, melted margarine and remaining ingredients; stir just until dry ingredients are moistened. Spread batter in prepared pan. Bake for 25 to 28 minutes, or until golden brown. Cool slightly before cutting.

Per Serving:

| | |
|---|---|
| Calories: | 285 |
| Protein: | 6 g. |
| Carbohydrate: | 29 g. |
| Fat: | 17 g. |
| Sodium: | 274 mg. |
| Cholesterol: | 47 mg. |

## Mushroom & Burgundy Steaks

1½-lb. boneless beef top round
   steak, about ¾ inch thick,
   trimmed and cut into
   serving-size pieces
1  pkg. (0.75 oz.) mushroom
   gravy mix
½  teaspoon dried marjoram
   leaves
¼  teaspoon dried thyme
   leaves
⅛  teaspoon garlic powder
⅓  cup thinly sliced celery
⅓  cup cubed carrot (¼-inch
   cubes)
1  small onion, cut into 8
   wedges
1  jar (4.5 oz.) sliced
   mushrooms, drained
¼  cup Burgundy wine
3  tablespoons water

4 to 6 servings

Pound each piece of beef to ¼-inch thickness. Set aside. In large plastic food-storage bag, combine gravy mix, marjoram, thyme and garlic powder. Add beef. Shake to coat. Arrange pieces in 10-inch square casserole. Top with celery, carrot, onion and mushrooms. Pour wine and water over vegetables. Cover. Microwave at High for 5 minutes. Microwave at 50% (Medium) for 35 to 40 minutes longer, or until beef is tender, turning pieces over and stirring sauce once. Let stand, covered, for 10 minutes.

| Per Serving: | |
| --- | --- |
| Calories: | 188 |
| Protein: | 26 g. |
| Carbohydrate: | 5 g. |
| Fat: | 6 g. |
| Sodium: | 366 mg. |
| Cholesterol: | 59 mg. |

---

### MENU

*Mushroom & Burgundy Steaks*
*Baked Potatoes*
*Light Green Salad with your choice of dressing\**

#### Time Management

• Conventionally bake potatoes while you microwave Mushroom & Burgundy Steaks. • Prepare and chill salad and dressing • Toss salad while beef stands.

## Baked Potatoes ▲

6  baking potatoes (10 to 12 oz.
   each)

6 servings

Heat conventional oven to 350°F. Pierce potatoes with fork. Place on oven rack. Bake for 1 hour to 1 hour 15 minutes, or until tender.

| Per Serving: | | | | |
| --- | --- | --- | --- | --- |
| Calories: | 374 | Fat: | | — |
| Protein: | 12 g. | Sodium: | | 45 mg. |
| Carbohydrate: | 84 g. | Cholesterol: | | — |

## MENU

*Beef Lo Mein*
*Fresh Pineapple Slices*\*

### Time Management

• Heat water for noodles conventionally while you cut up meat and vegetables. • Microwave meat, vegetables and sauce while noodles boil. • Combine Lo Mein ingredients and microwave while you prepare pineapple.

## Beef Lo Mein

5 oz. uncooked Chinese
   noodles or spaghetti
1 tablespoon vegetable oil
1-lb. boneless beef sirloin steak,
   about 1 inch thick, cut into
   thin strips
2 tablespoons oyster sauce
2 cups sliced bok choy, stems
   and leaves, ½-inch slices
1 cup diagonally sliced carrots,
   ⅛-inch slices
2 teaspoons cornstarch
1 teaspoon sugar
½ teaspoon ground ginger
¼ teaspoon crushed red
   pepper flakes
1 clove garlic, minced
⅓ cup water
3 tablespoons soy sauce
1 cup fresh pea pods
½ cup diagonally sliced green
   onions, ½-inch slices

4 to 6 servings

Prepare noodles as directed on package. Rinse and drain. Toss with oil. Cover to keep warm. Set aside. In 1-quart casserole, combine beef and oyster sauce. Cover. Microwave at High for 6 to 10 minutes, or until meat is no longer pink, stirring 3 or 4 times. Drain. Set aside. In 3-quart casserole, combine bok choy and carrots. Cover. Microwave at High for 4 to 6 minutes, or until vegetables are tender-crisp. Set aside.

In 2-cup measure, combine cornstarch, sugar, ginger, red pepper flakes and garlic. Blend in water and soy sauce. Microwave at High for 2 to 3 minutes, or until mixture is thickened and translucent, stirring every minute. Add to bok choy and carrot mixture. Stir in cooked noodles, beef, pea pods and green onions. Microwave at High for 5 to 6 minutes, or until hot, stirring once.

Per Serving:

| Calories: | 262 | Fat: | 8 g. |
|---|---|---|---|
| Protein: | 21 g. | Sodium: | 801 mg. |
| Carbohydrate: | 25 g. | Cholesterol: | 43 mg. |

*Whole Roasted Chicken with Harvest Vegetables*
*Country-style Biscuits*

**Time Management**

• Assemble chicken and vegetables. • While microwaving chicken, heat conventional oven and prepare biscuits. • Bake biscuits while chicken stands.

## Whole Roasted Chicken with Harvest Vegetables

| | |
|---|---|
| ½ teaspoon poultry seasoning | ½ lb. new potatoes, quartered |
| ¼ teaspoon paprika | 1 pint fresh Brussels sprouts, trimmed |
| ¼ teaspoon salt | |
| ⅛ teaspoon garlic powder | 3 medium carrots, cut into thirds |
| ⅛ teaspoon pepper | |
| 2½ to 3-lb. whole broiler-fryer chicken | 1 small onion, cut into 8 wedges |
| 1 tablespoon all-purpose flour | ¼ cup water |

4 servings

In small bowl, combine poultry seasoning, paprika, salt, garlic powder and pepper. Rub mixture evenly over chicken. Set aside. Place flour in nylon cooking bag. Shake to coat bag. Add seasoned chicken and remaining ingredients. Secure bag loosely with nylon tie or string. Place in 10-inch square casserole. Microwave at High for 25 to 30 minutes, or until legs move freely and juices run clear, rotating dish 2 or 3 times. Let bag stand, closed, for 10 minutes.

| Per Serving: | | | |
|---|---|---|---|
| Calories: | 288 | Fat: | 7 g. |
| Protein: | 30 g. | Sodium: | 250 mg. |
| Carbohydrate: | 26 g. | Cholesterol: | 81 mg. |

## Country-style Biscuits

| | |
|---|---|
| 2 cups buttermilk baking mix | 1 tablespoon dried parsley flakes |
| ½ cup small curd cottage cheese | |
| | ½ cup milk |

8 biscuits

Heat conventional oven to 450°F. In large mixing bowl, place all ingredients; blend just until moistened. Divide mixture into eighths. Drop onto ungreased baking sheet. Bake for 13 to 16 minutes, or until light golden brown.

| Per Serving: | | | |
|---|---|---|---|
| Calories: | 146 | Fat: | 5 g. |
| Protein: | 5 g. | Sodium: | 444 mg. |
| Carbohydrate: | 21 g. | Cholesterol: | 3 mg. |

**Time Management**

• At least 2 hours before serving, prepare coleslaw; chill. • About 45 minutes before serving, sauté chicken conventionally while you prepare rice. • Microwave sauce for chicken just before serving.

## Five-spice Honey Chicken ▶

⅓ cup all-purpose flour
2 teaspoons five-spice powder
½ teaspoon salt
3 bone-in whole chicken
　breasts (12 to 14 oz. each),
　split, skin removed
¼ cup peanut oil
½ cup cold water
1 tablespoon cornstarch

3 tablespoons honey
1 tablespoon plus 1½
　teaspoons lemon juice
1 tablespoon sugar
1 tablespoon catsup
1 teaspoon instant chicken
　bouillon granules
1 teaspoon soy sauce

4 to 6 servings

In large plastic food-storage bag, mix flour, five-spice powder and salt. Add chicken breast halves. Shake to coat. Discard any excess flour mixture. In 10-inch skillet, heat oil conventionally over medium-high heat until hot. Add chicken breasts. Brown. Reduce heat to low and cook until chicken is no longer pink and juices run clear, about 18 to 20 minutes. Set aside. In 2-cup measure, blend water and cornstarch. Stir in remaining ingredients. Microwave at High for 3 to 5 minutes, or until sauce is thickened and translucent, stirring 2 or 3 times. Pour sauce over chicken breasts. Garnish with lemon zest, if desired.

| Per Serving: | | | |
|---|---|---|---|
| Calories: | 345 | Fat: | 13 g. |
| Protein: | 36 g. | Sodium: | 408 mg. |
| Carbohydrate: | 19 g. | Cholesterol: | 96 mg. |

## White Rice ▶

2 cups hot water
1 cup uncooked long-grain
　white rice

1 tablespoon margarine or
　butter
½ teaspoon salt

6 to 8 servings

In 2-quart casserole, combine water, rice, margarine and salt. Cover. Microwave at High for 5 minutes. Microwave at 50% (Medium) for 12 to 15 minutes longer, or until rice is tender and liquid is absorbed. Let stand, covered, for 5 minutes.

| Per Serving: | | | |
|---|---|---|---|
| Calories: | 96 | Fat: | 1 g. |
| Protein: | 2 g. | Sodium: | 150 mg. |
| Carbohydrate: | 19 g. | Cholesterol: | — |

## Chinese Coleslaw ▶

¾ lb. Chinese cabbage (Napa)
⅔ cup shredded carrot
½ cup chopped green pepper
2 tablespoons sliced green
　onion

**Dressing:**
¼ cup vegetable oil
3 tablespoons sugar
2 tablespoons white vinegar
½ teaspoon salt
⅛ teaspoon white pepper
⅛ teaspoon sesame oil

4 to 6 servings

Remove and discard 1-inch portion from stem end of cabbage. Shred leafy portion and thinly slice stalk portion from each leaf (about 5 cups). In medium mixing bowl, combine cabbage, carrot, green pepper and onion. Set aside. In 2-cup measure, combine all dressing ingredients. Microwave at High for 1 to 1¾ minutes, or until dressing boils, stirring once. Stir to dissolve any remaining sugar. Pour hot dressing over cabbage mixture. Toss to coat. Cover and chill at least 1½ hours.

| Per Serving: | |
|---|---|
| Calories: | 123 |
| Protein: | 1 g. |
| Carbohydrate: | 10 g. |
| Fat: | 9 g. |
| Sodium: | 223 mg. |
| Cholesterol: | — |

## Herbed Turkey Meatloaf ▲

1½ lbs. ground turkey
 1 cup herb-seasoned stuffing
    mix
⅓ cup chopped onion
 1 egg
½ teaspoon dried parsley
    flakes
½ teaspoon seasoned salt

4 to 6 servings

Heat conventional oven to 350°F.
In medium mixing bowl, combine
all ingredients. Shape mixture into
loaf and place in 8 × 4-inch loaf
pan. Bake 1 hour 10 minutes to 1
hour 15 minutes, or until meatloaf
is firm and temperature in center
registers 185°F. Let stand for 5 to
10 minutes.

| Per Serving: | |
| --- | --- |
| Calories: | 248 |
| Protein: | 29 g. |
| Carbohydrate: | 18 g. |
| Fat: | 6 g. |
| Sodium: | 513 mg. |
| Cholesterol: | 111 mg. |

---

### MENU

*Herbed Turkey Meatloaf*
*Broccoli Rice Pilaf*

### Time Management

• About 1½ hours before serving, heat conventional oven and bake meatloaf. • When meatloaf has baked ½ hour, microwave rice pilaf.

## Broccoli Rice Pilaf ▲

¼ cup sliced almonds
 2 tablespoons margarine or
    butter
 1 cup fresh broccoli flowerets
 1 cup uncooked long-grain
    white rice

 1 can (14½ oz.) ready-to-serve
    chicken broth plus water to
    equal 2 cups
¼ teaspoon crushed red
    pepper flakes (optional)

4 to 6 servings

In 2-quart casserole, microwave almonds and margarine at High for 3
to 5 minutes, or until margarine is melted and almonds begin to brown.
Add broccoli and rice. Toss to coat with margarine. Add chicken broth
and red pepper flakes. Cover. Microwave at High for 5 minutes. Microwave at 50% (Medium) for 15 to 25 minutes longer, or until rice is tender
and liquid is absorbed. Let stand, covered, for 5 minutes.

| Per Serving: | | | |
| --- | --- | --- | --- |
| Calories: | 184 | Fat: | 6 g. |
| Protein: | 5 g. | Sodium: | 265 mg. |
| Carbohydrate: | 27 g. | Cholesterol: | — |

## MENU

*Deli Divan*

*Fresh
Strawberry-Banana Salad*

### Time Management

• Heat conventional oven while you toast bread and microwave broccoli and sauce. • Assemble divan. • While divan bakes, prepare salad. Toss salad just before serving.

## Deli Divan

6  to 8 slices French bread (½-
   inch thick slices), toasted
1  pkg. (10 oz.) frozen chopped
   broccoli
2  tablespoons water
1  pkg. (0.87 oz.) white sauce
   mix
   Dash pepper
   Dash ground nutmeg
1  cup milk
½  cup sour cream
1  jar (2.5 oz.) sliced
   mushrooms, drained
¾  lb. thinly sliced fully cooked
   turkey
1  cup shredded Cheddar
   cheese
¼  cup sliced almonds

4 to 6 servings

Heat conventional oven to 325°F. Arrange toast slices in single layer in 12 × 8-inch baking dish. Set aside. Place broccoli and water in 1-quart casserole. Cover. Microwave at High for 4 to 6 minutes, or until broccoli is hot, stirring once to break apart. Drain. Set aside. In 4-cup measure, combine white sauce mix, pepper and nutmeg. Blend in milk. Microwave at High for 4 to 6 minutes, or until mixture thickens and bubbles, stirring with whisk 2 or 3 times. Blend in sour cream. Set aside. Sprinkle broccoli and mushrooms in an even layer over toast. Top with one-half of sauce. Layer turkey over sauce. Sprinkle with cheese. Spread top with remaining sauce. Sprinkle with almonds. Bake for 20 to 25 minutes, or until hot.

| Per Serving: | | | |
|---|---|---|---|
| Calories: | 399 | Fat: | 19 g. |
| Protein: | 29 g. | Sodium: | 586 mg. |
| Carbohydrate: | 28 g. | Cholesterol: | 76 mg. |

## Fresh Strawberry-Banana Salad

4  cups torn Bibb lettuce
1  cup sliced banana
1  cup quartered fresh
   strawberries
2  tablespoons pineapple juice
1  tablespoon plus 1½
   teaspoons vegetable oil
1  tablespoon honey
½  teaspoon poppy seed
¼  teaspoon dry mustard

4 to 6 servings

In medium mixing bowl or salad bowl, combine lettuce, banana and strawberries. Set aside. In 1-cup measure, blend remaining ingredients. Pour over lettuce and fruit. Toss to coat. Serve immediately.

| Per Serving: | |
|---|---|
| Calories: | 81 |
| Protein: | 1 g. |
| Carbohydrate: | 12 g. |
| Fat: | 4 g. |
| Sodium: | 3 mg. |
| Cholesterol: | — |

## ◄ Southern-style Chicken Pot Pie

- 1 pkg. (10 oz.) frozen lima beans
- 2/3 cup thinly sliced carrot
- 1/3 cup chopped onion
- 1/2 cup water
- 3/4 teaspoon dried rubbed sage leaves
- 1/4 teaspoon salt
- 1/8 teaspoon pepper
- 2 cups fresh cauliflowerets
- 1 1/2 cups cubed cooked chicken (3/4-inch cubes)
- 1 can (10 3/4 oz.) condensed cream of chicken soup

**Topping:**
- 2/3 cup all-purpose flour
- 1/3 cup yellow cornmeal
- 1 teaspoon sugar
- 3/4 teaspoon baking soda
- 1/8 teaspoon salt
- 1/3 cup margarine or butter
- 3/4 cup buttermilk

4 to 6 servings

Heat conventional oven to 425°F. In 2-quart casserole or soufflé dish, combine lima beans, carrot, onion, water, sage, salt and pepper. Cover. Microwave at High for 9 to 12 minutes, or until vegetables are tender, stirring 2 or 3 times. Add cauliflowerets. Re-cover. Microwave at High for 3 to 4 minutes, or until tender-crisp. Add chicken and soup. Mix well. Set aside. In small mixing bowl, combine flour, cornmeal, sugar, baking soda and salt. In 1-cup measure, microwave margarine at High for 1 1/2 to 1 3/4 minutes, or until melted. Add margarine and buttermilk to flour mixture; blend just until moistened. Spread batter evenly over chicken mixture. Bake for 15 to 20 minutes, or until top is golden brown.

Per Serving:

| | |
|---|---|
| Calories: | 375 |
| Protein: | 21 g. |
| Carbohydrate: | 34 g. |
| Fat: | 17 g. |
| Sodium: | 881 mg. |
| Cholesterol: | 43 mg. |

---

### MENU

*Southern-style Chicken Pot Pie*
*Garden Favorites*

#### Time Management

• Heat conventional oven while you microwave vegetables for pie and mix cornmeal topping. • Assemble pie and bake while microwaving Garden Favorites.

## Garden Favorites ▲

- 2 medium ears fresh corn on the cob
- 2 tablespoons water
- 2 medium tomatoes, each cut into 6 wedges
- 2 tablespoons margarine or butter
- 1/2 teaspoon dried basil leaves
- 1/2 teaspoon Dijon mustard

4 to 6 servings

Remove husk and silk from corn. Cut each ear into 2-inch lengths. Place in 2-quart casserole. Sprinkle with water. Cover. Microwave at High for 5 to 7 minutes, or until corn is tender. Drain. Add tomatoes. Re-cover. Microwave at High for 1 to 1 1/2 minutes, or until tomatoes are hot. Set aside. In 1-cup measure, combine margarine and basil. Microwave at High for 45 seconds to 1 minute, or until margarine is melted. Stir in Dijon mustard. Pour evenly over hot corn and tomatoes.

Per Serving:

| | | | |
|---|---|---|---|
| Calories: | 63 | Fat: | 4 g. |
| Protein: | 1 g. | Sodium: | 63 mg. |
| Carbohydrate: | 6 g. | Cholesterol: | — |

## Cacciatore Casserole

### MENU

*Cacciatore Casserole*
*Light Green Salad*
*with Croutons*
*& your choice of dressing\**
*Garlic Toast\**

### Time Management

• Prepare and chill salad and dressing. • Cook pasta conventionally while you microwave vegetables. • Assemble casserole; microwave. • Toss salad just before serving.

2½  cups uncooked rotini pasta
1½  cups sliced fresh
      mushrooms
½  cup thinly sliced carrot
⅓  cup chopped onion
⅓  cup chopped green pepper
1  tablespoon vegetable oil

2  teaspoons dried parsley
    flakes, divided
1½  cups cubed cooked chicken
      (¾-inch cubes)
1  jar (15½ oz.) spaghetti
    sauce without meat
1  cup shredded mozzarella
    cheese

4 to 6 servings

Prepare pasta as directed on package. Rinse and drain. Set aside. In 2-quart casserole, combine mushrooms, carrot, onion, pepper, oil and 1 teaspoon parsley flakes. Cover. Microwave at High for 5 to 7 minutes, or until carrot is tender, stirring once or twice. Add cooked rotini to vegetables. Add chicken and spaghetti sauce. Mix well. Re-cover. Microwave at High for 6 to 7 minutes, or until hot, stirring once. Sprinkle casserole with cheese and remaining 1 teaspoon parsley flakes. Microwave, uncovered, at High for 1½ to 2 minutes, or until cheese is melted.

Per Serving:
| | | | |
|---|---|---|---|
| Calories: | 373 | Fat: | 12 g. |
| Protein: | 22 g. | Sodium: | 498 mg. |
| Carbohydrate: | 44 g. | Cholesterol: | 41 mg. |

# New Mexican Meatloaf

### MENU

*New Mexican Meatloaf*
*Jalapeño Cheddar Potatoes*
*Southwestern Salad*

### Time Management

• Heat conventional oven while you prepare meatloaf. • Bake meatloaf; prepare and chill salad and dressing. • When meatloaf has cooked 35 to 45 minutes, microwave potatoes and sauce.

**Meatloaf:**
¼ cup finely chopped onion
¼ cup finely chopped green pepper
1 clove garlic, minced
¾ lb. lean ground beef
¾ lb. bulk mild pork sausage
½ cup unseasoned dry bread crumbs

½ cup tomato juice
2 eggs

**Topping:**
3 tablespoons taco sauce
1 tablespoon packed dark brown sugar
½ teaspoon prepared mustard

4 to 6 servings

Heat conventional oven to 350°F. In medium mixing bowl, combine onion, green pepper and garlic. Microwave at High for 2 to 2½ minutes, or until vegetables are tender. Add remaining meatloaf ingredients. Mix well. Shape into an 8 × 4-inch loaf. Place on conventional broiler pan, or on rack in roasting pan. Set aside. In small dish, blend all topping ingredients. Spoon evenly over top of loaf. Bake for 1 hour to 1 hour 10 minutes, or until internal temperature registers 165°F. Let stand for 10 minutes.

| Per Serving: | | | |
|---|---|---|---|
| Calories: | 300 | Fat: | 17 g. |
| Protein: | 24 g. | Sodium: | 598 mg. |
| Carbohydrate: | 11 g. | Cholesterol: | 167 mg. |

## Jalapeño Cheddar Potatoes

1½  lbs. potatoes, sliced (¼-inch slices)
½  cup chopped red or green pepper
1  to 2 tablespoons fresh or canned sliced jalapeño peppers
¼  cup water

2  tablespoons margarine or butter
2  tablespoons all-purpose flour
¼  teaspoon salt
1  cup half-and-half
1  cup shredded sharp Cheddar cheese

4 to 6 servings

In 2-quart casserole, combine potatoes, red pepper, jalapeño peppers and water. Cover. Microwave at High for 10 to 14 minutes, or until potatoes are fork-tender, stirring once or twice. Drain. Set aside. In 4-cup measure, microwave margarine at High for 45 seconds to 1 minute, or until melted. Stir in flour and salt. Blend in half-and-half. Microwave at High for 5 to 9 minutes, or until sauce thickens and bubbles, stirring 2 or 3 times. Stir in cheese until melted. Pour cheese sauce over potatoes. Toss to coat.

| Per Serving: | | | |
|---|---|---|---|
| Calories: | 275 | Fat: | 15 g. |
| Protein: | 8 g. | Sodium: | 295 mg. |
| Carbohydrate: | 28 g. | Cholesterol: | 35 mg. |

## Southwestern Salad

**Salad:**
6  cups torn lettuce (combination of Bibb, iceberg, leaf or romaine)
1  medium carrot, shredded
1  small avocado, peeled and sliced
½  cup julienne jicama (2 × ¼-inch strips)
2  tablespoons sliced green onion
2  tablespoons sliced pitted black olives (optional)

**Dressing:**
⅓  cup olive or vegetable oil
3  tablespoons red wine vinegar
1  teaspoon dried cilantro leaves
½  teaspoon ground cumin
¼  teaspoon garlic salt

4 to 6 servings

Place lettuce in large mixing bowl or salad bowl. Add remaining salad ingredients. Toss gently to combine. Set aside. In 1-cup measure, place all dressing ingredients. Mix well. Just before serving, pour over greens. Toss to coat.

| Per Serving: | |
|---|---|
| Calories: | 190 |
| Protein: | 2 g. |
| Carbohydrate: | 7 g. |
| Fat: | 18 g. |
| Sodium: | 102 mg. |
| Cholesterol: | — |

| Ham & Sweet Potato Scallop | Broccoli Spears with Mustard Sauce |
|---|---|

### Time Management

• Begin microwaving Ham & Sweet Potato Scallop. • Add sauce and cover with foil; set aside for about 5 minutes. • Start microwaving broccoli. • Discard foil; sprinkle scallop with topping and brown under conventional broiler.

## Ham & Sweet Potato Scallop ▶

**Topping:**
2 tablespoons margarine or butter
⅓ cup unseasoned dry bread crumbs
¼ cup chopped pecans
1 tablespoon snipped fresh parsley

3 medium potatoes (about 1 lb.), thinly sliced
¼ cup water

2 cups fully cooked cubed ham (½-inch cubes)
1 can (23 oz.) sweet potatoes, drained
⅓ cup sliced green onions

**Sauce:**
2 tablespoons margarine or butter
¼ cup all-purpose flour
½ teaspoon salt
¼ teaspoon dry mustard

⅛ teaspoon white pepper
2 cups milk
1 tablespoon snipped fresh parsley

4 to 6 servings

Per Serving:
| | |
|---|---|
| Calories: | 391 |
| Protein: | 17 g. |
| Carbohydrate: | 46 g. |
| Fat: | 16 g. |
| Sodium: | 955 mg. |
| Cholesterol: | 31 mg. |

## How to Microwave Ham & Sweet Potato Scallop

**Microwave** 2 tablespoons margarine in small mixing bowl at High for 45 seconds to 1 minute, or until melted. Add remaining topping ingredients. Mix well. Set aside. In 10-inch square casserole, place potatoes and water. Cover. Microwave at High for 8 to 14 minutes, or until tender, stirring once. Drain.

**Add** ham, sweet potatoes and onions. Cover with plastic wrap. Set aside. In 4-cup measure, microwave 2 tablespoons margarine at High for 45 seconds to 1 minute, or until melted. Stir in flour and seasonings. Blend in milk. Microwave at High for 6 to 9½ minutes, or until mixture thickens and bubbles, stirring after the first 2 minutes and then every minute. Add parsley. Set aside.

**Microwave** ham and potato mixture, covered, at High for 4 to 6 minutes, or until hot. Pour white sauce evenly over potato mixture. Stir gently to coat. Sprinkle with topping mixture. Place under conventional broiler 4 to 5 inches from heat until lightly browned, about 4 minutes.

## Broccoli Spears with Mustard Sauce ▲

2 pkgs. (10 oz. each) frozen
    broccoli spears
¼ cup water
3 tablespoons margarine or
    butter
2 teaspoons coarse brown
    mustard
½ teaspoon sugar
⅛ teaspoon salt

       4 to 6 servings

In 10-inch square casserole, combine broccoli and water. Cover. Microwave at High for 9 to 12 minutes, or until broccoli is tender, stirring twice. Drain. Set aside. In 1-cup measure, microwave margarine at High for 45 seconds to 1 minute, or until melted. Blend in remaining ingredients. Pour over broccoli spears.

Per Serving:

| | | | |
|---|---|---|---|
| Calories: | 77 | Fat: | 6 g. |
| Protein: | 3 g. | Sodium: | 153 mg. |
| Carbohydrate: | 5 g. | Cholesterol: | — |

# Peppered Pork & Vegetables with Soft Noodles

8 oz. uncooked medium egg
  noodles
3 tablespoons vegetable oil,
  divided
1 cup diagonally sliced celery
  (¼-inch slices)
½ cup red or green pepper
  chunks (¾-inch chunks)
⅓ cup coarsely chopped onion
1 jar (7 oz.) sliced shiitake
  mushrooms, drained
1 jar (7 oz.) whole baby corn,
  drained
⅛ teaspoon sesame oil

1 lb. butterflied pork chops,
  trimmed and cut into thin
  strips

**Sauce:**
½ cup ready-to-serve chicken
  broth
¼ cup teriyaki sauce
1 tablespoon plus 1½
  teaspoons cornstarch
¼ teaspoon pepper
¼ teaspoon sesame oil
⅛ teaspoon instant minced
  garlic

4 to 6 servings

Per Serving:
| | | | |
|---|---|---|---|
| Calories: | 402 | Fat: | 15 g. |
| Protein: | 25 g. | Sodium: | 302 mg. |
| Carbohydrate: | 41 g. | Cholesterol: | 91 mg. |

## How to Make Peppered Pork & Vegetables with Soft Noodles

**Prepare** egg noodles as directed on package. Rinse and drain. Toss with 1 tablespoon vegetable oil. Cover to keep warm. Set aside.

**Combine** celery, red pepper, onion and 1 tablespoon vegetable oil in 3-quart casserole. Cover. Microwave at High for 3 to 4 minutes, or until vegetables are tender-crisp, stirring once.

**Stir** in mushrooms and corn. Set aside. In 10-inch skillet, heat remaining 1 tablespoon vegetable oil and ⅛ teaspoon sesame oil conventionally over medium-high heat.

**Add** pork strips. Stir-fry until meat is no longer pink, about 3 to 5 minutes. Add pork strips to vegetable mixture. Set aside.

**Combine** all sauce ingredients in 2-cup measure. Mix well. Microwave at High for 2 to 3½ minutes, or until sauce is thickened and translucent, stirring twice.

**Stir** sauce into pork and vegetables. Add cooked egg noodles. Toss to combine. Cover. Microwave at High for 1 to 2 minutes, or until hot.

# Mandarin Orange Gelatin Squares

Vegetable cooking spray
2 cups hot water
1 pkg. (0.6 oz.) low-calorie orange-flavored gelatin
1½ cups orange juice
1 can (11 oz.) mandarin orange segments, drained
1 cup prepared whipped topping
½ cup plain low-fat yogurt

9 servings

Lightly spray 9-inch square baking dish with vegetable cooking spray. Set aside. Place water in 4-cup measure. Cover with plastic wrap. Microwave at High for 4 to 5 minutes, or until boiling. Place gelatin in medium mixing bowl. Add boiling water. Stir to dissolve gelatin. Mix in orange juice. Chill until gelatin is soft-set, about 1½ hours. Reserve 18 mandarin orange segments for garnish. Arrange remaining orange segments evenly in prepared dish. Reserve ½ cup soft-set gelatin and place in small mixing bowl. Set aside. Spoon remaining soft-set gelatin over orange segments in dish. Set aside. Blend whipped topping and yogurt into the reserved gelatin. Spoon over gelatin and orange segments. Arrange reserved orange segments on top (2 segments per serving). Chill at least 3 hours, or until set.

Per Serving:
| | | | |
|---|---|---|---|
| Calories: | 62 | Fat: | 1 g. |
| Protein: | 1 g. | Sodium: | 103 mg. |
| Carbohydrate: | 11 g. | Cholesterol: | 2 mg. |

## Caraway-buttered Egg Noodles ▶

4 cups uncooked wide egg noodles
¼ cup margarine or butter
1½ to 2 teaspoons caraway seed

¼ teaspoon salt
⅛ teaspoon white pepper
⅛ teaspoon onion powder

4 to 6 servings

Prepare egg noodles as directed on package. Rinse and drain. Cover to keep warm. Set aside. In 2-cup measure, microwave margarine at High for 1¼ to 1½ minutes, or until melted. Add remaining ingredients, except cooked egg noodles. Mix well. Place cooked egg noodles in serving bowl. Pour margarine mixture over noodles. Toss to coat.

| Per Serving: | | | | | |
|---|---|---|---|---|---|
| Calories: | 174 | Fat: | | 9 g. |
| Protein: | 4 g. | Sodium: | | 180 mg. |
| Carbohydrate: | 20 g. | Cholesterol: | | 25 mg. |

## Apple-buttered Brussels Sprouts ▶

2 pkgs. (10 oz. each) frozen Brussels sprouts
2 tablespoons water
¼ cup apple jelly

1 tablespoon margarine or butter
¼ teaspoon grated lemon peel

4 to 6 servings

In 2-quart casserole, place Brussels sprouts and water. Cover. Microwave at High for 10 to 13 minutes, or until hot, stirring twice to break apart. Drain. Cover to keep warm. Set aside. In 1-cup measure, combine remaining ingredients. Microwave at High for 1 to 1¼ minutes, or until jelly is melted, stirring every 30 seconds. Stir to melt margarine. Pour mixture over Brussels sprouts. Toss to coat.

| Per Serving: | | | | | |
|---|---|---|---|---|---|
| Calories: | 92 | Fat: | | 2 g. |
| Protein: | 4 g. | Sodium: | | 33 mg. |
| Carbohydrate: | 17 g. | Cholesterol: | | — |

## Bavarian Pork Chops ▶

3 tablespoons all-purpose flour
1 teaspoon ground cinnamon
¼ teaspoon ground allspice
¼ teaspoon salt
4 pork loin chops (5 to 6 oz. each), about ¾ inch thick
2 tablespoons vegetable oil
1 small red apple, cut into thin wedges
1 small green apple, cut into thin wedges
1 small onion, thinly sliced and separated into rings

**Sauce:**
¼ cup packed dark brown sugar
¼ teaspoon ground cinnamon
⅛ teaspoon salt
2 tablespoons apple juice
2 teaspoons cider vinegar

4 servings

In large plastic food-storage bag, combine flour, 1 teaspoon cinnamon, the allspice and ¼ teaspoon salt. Add pork chops. Shake to coat. Discard any excess flour. In 10-inch skillet, heat oil conventionally over medium-high heat until hot. Add pork chops. Brown both sides. Arrange chops in 9-inch square baking dish. Top with apple slices and onion. Set aside. In small bowl, mix brown sugar, ¼ teaspoon cinnamon and ⅛ teaspoon salt. Stir in apple juice and vinegar. Pour evenly over pork chop mixture. Cover with wax paper. Microwave at 70% (Medium High) for 12 to 17 minutes, or until pork near bone is no longer pink, rotating dish once or twice. Let stand, covered, for 5 to 10 minutes.

| Per Serving: | |
|---|---|
| Calories: | 469 |
| Protein: | 34 g. |
| Carbohydrate: | 29 g. |
| Fat: | 24 g. |
| Sodium: | 282 mg. |
| Cholesterol: | 107 mg. |

## How to Microwave Louisana Pork Roast

## Louisiana Pork Roast

| | | | |
| --- | --- | --- | --- |
| 1 | teaspoon ground thyme | 2½ | to 3-lb. boneless pork loin roast |
| 1 | teaspoon paprika | 2 | cloves garlic, each cut into 6 slivers |
| ½ | teaspoon ground cumin | | |
| ½ | teaspoon dry mustard | 1 | tablespoon all-purpose flour |
| ½ | teaspoon black pepper | 2 | tablespoons water |
| ½ | teaspoon cayenne | | |
| ¼ | teaspoon white pepper | | |

6 servings

| Per Serving: | | | |
| --- | --- | --- | --- |
| Calories: | 338 | Fat: | 15 g. |
| Protein: | 46 g. | Sodium: | 111 mg. |
| Carbohydrate: | 2 g. | Cholesterol: | 139 mg. |

**Combine** all seasonings in small bowl. Mix well. Set aside. Randomly cut slits in roast and insert 1 garlic sliver in each slit. Rub seasoning mixture onto roast surface.

**Place** flour in nylon cooking bag. Shake to coat bag. Add seasoned pork roast. Sprinkle with water. Secure bag loosely with nylon tie or string.

**Place** in 9-inch square baking dish. Estimate total cooking time at 17 to 20 minutes per pound. Divide total cooking time in half. Microwave at High for first 5 minutes. Microwave at 50% (Medium) for remainder of first half of time.

**Turn** roast over. Microwave at 50% (Medium) for second half of time, or until internal temperature registers 165°F in several places. Let bag stand, closed, for 15 minutes.

80

## Black-eyed Peas & Peppers

1 pkg. (10 oz.) frozen black-
    eyed peas
¾ cup chopped onion
½ cup chopped red pepper
½ cup chopped green pepper
¼ cup thinly sliced celery
1 tablespoon olive oil
½ teaspoon dried rubbed sage
    leaves
¼ teaspoon seasoned salt
⅛ teaspoon cayenne

        4 to 6 servings

Prepare peas conventionally as directed on package. Drain. Set aside. In 1-quart casserole, combine remaining ingredients. Cover. Microwave at High for 4 to 6 minutes, or until vegetables are tender, stirring once. Stir in peas.

| Per Serving: | | | |
|---|---|---|---|
| Calories: | 89 | Fat: | 3 g. |
| Protein: | 4 g. | Sodium: | 73 mg. |
| Carbohydrate: | 13 g. | Cholesterol: | — |

## ◄ Lamb & Spinach-stuffed Manicotti

 8  uncooked manicotti shells
 ½  lb. ground lamb
 ¼  cup chopped onion
 1  clove garlic, minced
 ¼  teaspoon salt
 ⅛  teaspoon pepper
 1  pkg. (10 oz.) frozen chopped spinach
 ¾  cup ricotta cheese
 ½  cup shredded mozzarella cheese
 1  egg
 1  teaspoon dried oregano leaves
 1  pkg. (0.87 oz.) white sauce mix
 1  cup milk

4 to 6 servings

Heat conventional oven to 350°F. Prepare manicotti as directed on package. Rinse and drain. Set aside. In 2-quart casserole, combine lamb, onion, garlic, salt and pepper. Cover. Microwave at High for 4 to 6 minutes, or until meat is no longer pink, stirring 2 or 3 times to break apart. Drain. Set aside. Place spinach in 1-quart casserole. Microwave at High for 4 to 6 minutes, or until spinach is defrosted. Drain, pressing to remove excess moisture. Add spinach, ricotta, mozzarella, egg and oregano to lamb mixture. Mix well. Stuff each cooked manicotti shell with scant ½ cup lamb mixture. Arrange stuffed shells in even layer in 12 × 8-inch baking dish. Set aside. Place white sauce mix in 4-cup measure. Blend in milk. Microwave at High for 4 to 6 minutes, or until mixture thickens and bubbles, stirring 2 or 3 times. Pour sauce over stuffed manicotti shells. Cover with foil. Bake for 30 to 35 minutes, or until hot.

| Per Serving: | |
| --- | --- |
| Calories: | 267 |
| Protein: | 21 g. |
| Carbohydrate: | 25 g. |
| Fat: | 9 g. |
| Sodium: | 396 mg. |
| Cholesterol: | 92 mg. |

---

## Rosemary-buttered Summer Squash ▲

1 medium zucchini, cut in half lengthwise and sliced (¼-inch slices)
1 medium summer squash, cut in half lengthwise and sliced (¼-inch slices)

2 tablespoons margarine or butter
½ teaspoon dried rosemary leaves, crushed
¼ teaspoon garlic salt

4 to 6 servings

Place all ingredients in 2-quart casserole. Cover. Microwave at High for 8 to 10 minutes, or until squash is tender, stirring once.

| Per Serving: | | | |
| --- | --- | --- | --- |
| Calories: | 42 | Fat: | 4 g. |
| Protein: | 1 g. | Sodium: | 123 mg. |
| Carbohydrate: | 2 g. | Cholesterol: | — |

**MENU**

*Broiled Lamb Chops*
*Summer Vegetable Medley*
*Crusty Rolls\**

**Time Management**

• Prepare chops and vegetables for cooking. • Microwave vegetables while you broil chops conventionally.

## Broiled Lamb Chops ▶

4 lamb loin chops (4 to 5 oz. each)
¼ cup margarine or butter
1 teaspoon Dijon mustard
1 tablespoon snipped fresh parsley
1 clove garlic, minced

4 servings

Secure tail ends of chops around meaty portion of chops with wooden picks. Place lamb chops on conventional broiler pan. In small bowl, microwave margarine at High for 1¼ to 1½ minutes, or until melted. Blend in mustard. Stir in parsley and garlic. Brush lamb chops with margarine mixture. Place under conventional broiler, 3 to 4 inches from heat. Broil for 5 to 7 minutes on each side, or until desired doneness, basting with margarine mixture several times during cooking.

Per Serving:
| | |
|---|---|
| Calories: | 262 |
| Protein: | 24 g. |
| Carbohydrate: | — |
| Fat: | 18 g. |
| Sodium: | 230 mg. |
| Cholesterol: | 85 mg. |

## Summer Vegetable Medley ▲

2 cups fresh baby carrots (about 12 oz.)
2 tablespoons water
1 cup fresh mushrooms, cut in half
1 cup fresh pea pods
1 cup thinly sliced zucchini
½ cup thinly sliced radishes
2 tablespoons margarine or butter
2 teaspoons lemon juice
½ teaspoon salt

4 to 6 servings

In 2-quart casserole, combine carrots and water. Cover. Microwave at High for 4 minutes. Add remaining vegetables. Mix well. Re-cover. Microwave at High for 3 to 5 minutes, or until vegetables are tender-crisp. Drain. In small bowl, microwave margarine at High for 45 seconds to 1 minute, or until melted. Stir in lemon juice and salt. Pour margarine mixture over vegetables. Toss to coat.

Per Serving:
| | | | |
|---|---|---|---|
| Calories: | 73 | Fat: | 4 g. |
| Protein: | 2 g. | Sodium: | 250 mg. |
| Carbohydrate: | 9 g. | Cholesterol: | — |

*Pasta Pizza*
*Light Green Salad with Oil & Vinegar Dressing*

### Time Management

• Prepare and chill salad and dressing. • Boil and then fry pasta conventionally while you microwave sauce. • Assemble and microwave pizza. • Toss salad.

## Pasta Pizza

8 oz. uncooked angel hair spaghetti or capellini
2 tablespoons vegetable oil
⅓ cup chopped green pepper
¼ cup chopped onion
½ cup pizza sauce

¼ cup sliced pitted black olives (optional)
1 cup shredded mozzarella or Provolone cheese
¼ teaspoon Italian seasoning

4 to 6 servings

Prepare angel hair spaghetti as directed on package. Rinse and drain. In 9-inch nonstick skillet, heat oil conventionally over medium-high heat. Add cooked pasta, pressing into an even layer. Cook for about 4 to 5 minutes, or until golden brown. Invert pasta onto serving plate, browned-side-up. Set aside. In 1-quart casserole, combine green pepper and onion. Microwave at High for 2 to 3 minutes, or until tender. Set aside. Spread pizza sauce evenly over noodles. Top with green pepper, onion and olives. Sprinkle with cheese and Italian seasoning. Microwave at 70% (Medium High) for 3 to 4 minutes, or until cheese is melted, rotating plate once. Cut into wedges.

| Per Serving: | | | |
|---|---|---|---|
| Calories: | 249 | Fat: | 9 g. |
| Protein: | 10 g. | Sodium: | 213 mg. |
| Carbohydrate: | 32 g. | Cholesterol: | 10 mg. |

## Light Green Salad with Oil & Vinegar Dressing

**Salad:**
6 cups torn lettuce (combination of Bibb, iceberg, leaf or romaine)
1 medium carrot, shredded
1 medium tomato, cut into 8 wedges
2 tablespoons sliced green onion
½ cup seasoned croutons

**Dressing:**
⅓ cup olive or vegetable oil
3 tablespoons red wine vinegar
1 tablespoon snipped fresh parsley
¼ teaspoon garlic salt
¼ teaspoon Italian seasoning
⅛ teaspoon pepper

4 to 6 servings

Place lettuce in large mixing bowl or salad bowl. Add remaining salad ingredients. Toss gently to combine. Set aside. In 1-cup measure, place all dressing ingredients. Mix well. Just before serving, pour over salad. Toss to coat.

| Per Serving: | | | |
|---|---|---|---|
| Calories: | 156 | Fat: | 13 g. |
| Protein: | 2 g. | Sodium: | 176 mg. |
| Carbohydrate: | 8 g. | Cholesterol: | — |

## MENU

*Baked Mostaccioli with Three Cheeses*
*Light Green Salad with Cucumber-Dill Dressing*

### Time Management

• Heat conventional oven while you boil pasta on stove top and microwave sauce. • Combine pasta and sauce. • While pasta bakes conventionally, prepare salad and dressing; toss just before serving.

## Baked Mostaccioli with Three Cheeses

8 oz. uncooked mostaccioli
2 tablespoons margarine or butter
¼ cup all-purpose flour
½ teaspoon dried basil leaves
½ teaspoon salt
⅛ teaspoon pepper
2 cups milk
1¼ cups shredded Cheddar cheese, divided
1 cup shredded Monterey Jack cheese
½ cup fresh shredded Parmesan cheese, divided
1 medium tomato, sliced (6 slices)

4 to 6 servings

Heat conventional oven to 375°F. Prepare mostaccioli as directed on package. Rinse and drain. Set aside. In 2-quart soufflé dish or 2-quart casserole, microwave margarine at High for 45 seconds to 1 minute, or until melted. Stir in flour, basil, salt and pepper. Blend in milk. Microwave at High for 6 to 10 minutes, or until mixture thickens and bubbles, stirring with whisk every 2 minutes. Stir in 1 cup Cheddar cheese, the Monterey Jack cheese and ¼ cup Parmesan cheese. Stir to melt cheeses. Stir in cooked mostaccioli. Arrange tomato slices on top of pasta mixture. Sprinkle with remaining ¼ cup Cheddar and ¼ cup Parmesan cheeses. Bake for 30 to 35 minutes, or until bubbly and lightly browned around edges.

Per Serving:

| | | | |
|---|---|---|---|
| Calories: | 439 | Fat: | 22 g. |
| Protein: | 22 g. | Sodium: | 667 mg. |
| Carbohydrate: | 38 g. | Cholesterol: | 54 mg. |

# Light Green Salad with Cucumber-Dill Dressing

## Dressing:
⅓ cup mayonnaise
⅓ cup plain yogurt
½ teaspoon sugar
¼ teaspoon dried dill weed
¼ teaspoon garlic salt
⅓ cup seeded coarsely
    chopped cucumber

## Salad:
6 cups torn lettuce
   (combination of Bibb,
   iceberg, leaf or romaine)
1 medium carrot, shredded
1 medium tomato, cut into 8
   wedges
2 tablespoons sliced green
   onion
½ cup seasoned croutons

4 to 6 servings

In small mixing bowl, combine
mayonnaise, yogurt, sugar, dill
weed and garlic salt. Mix well.
Stir in cucumber. Cover and chill
until serving time. Place lettuce
in large mixing bowl or salad
bowl. Add remaining salad ingredients. Toss gently to combine.
Serve salad with dressing.

| Per Serving: | |
| --- | --- |
| Calories: | 132 |
| Protein: | 2 g. |
| Carbohydrate: | 8 g. |
| Fat: | 10 g. |
| Sodium: | 213 mg. |
| Cholesterol: | 8 mg. |

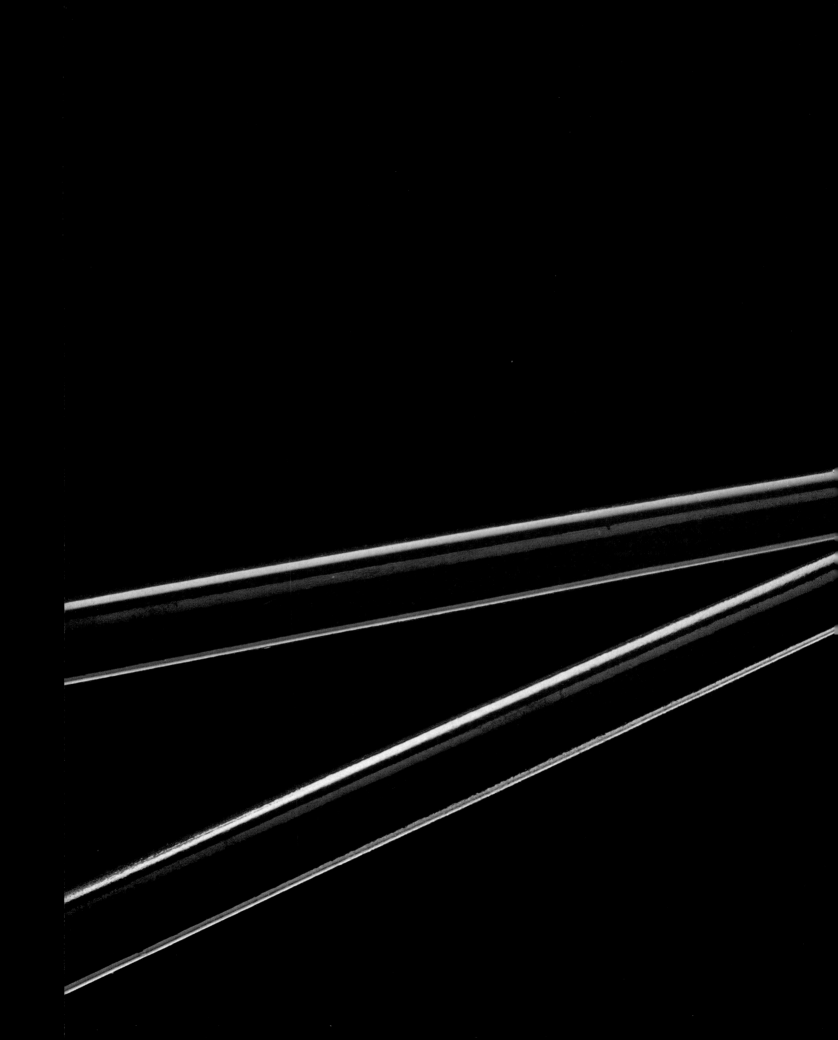

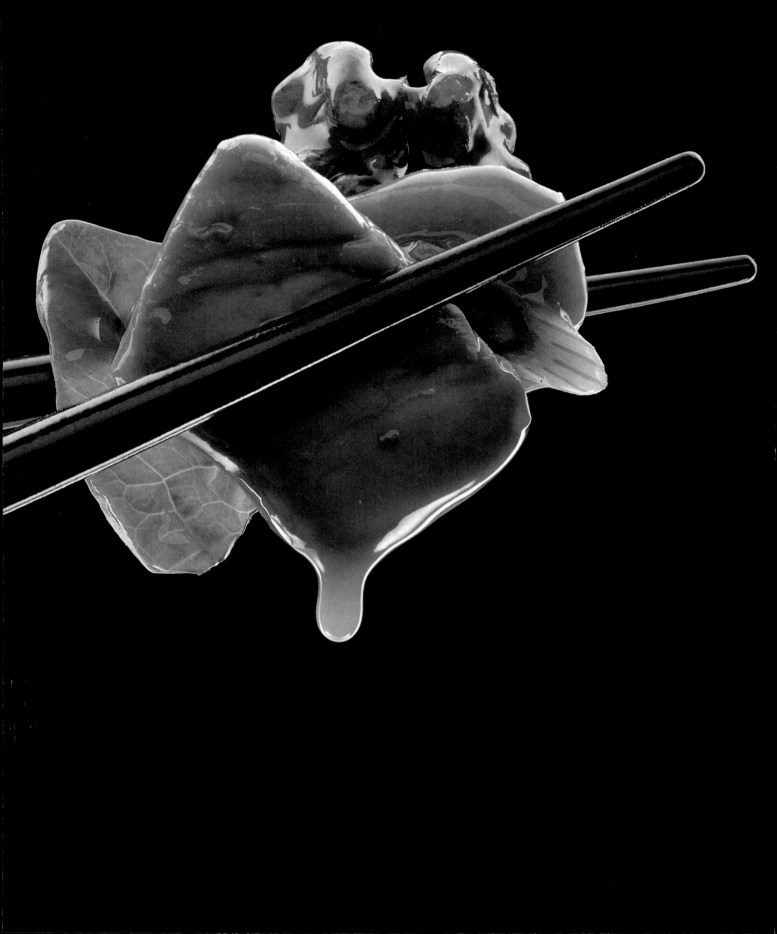

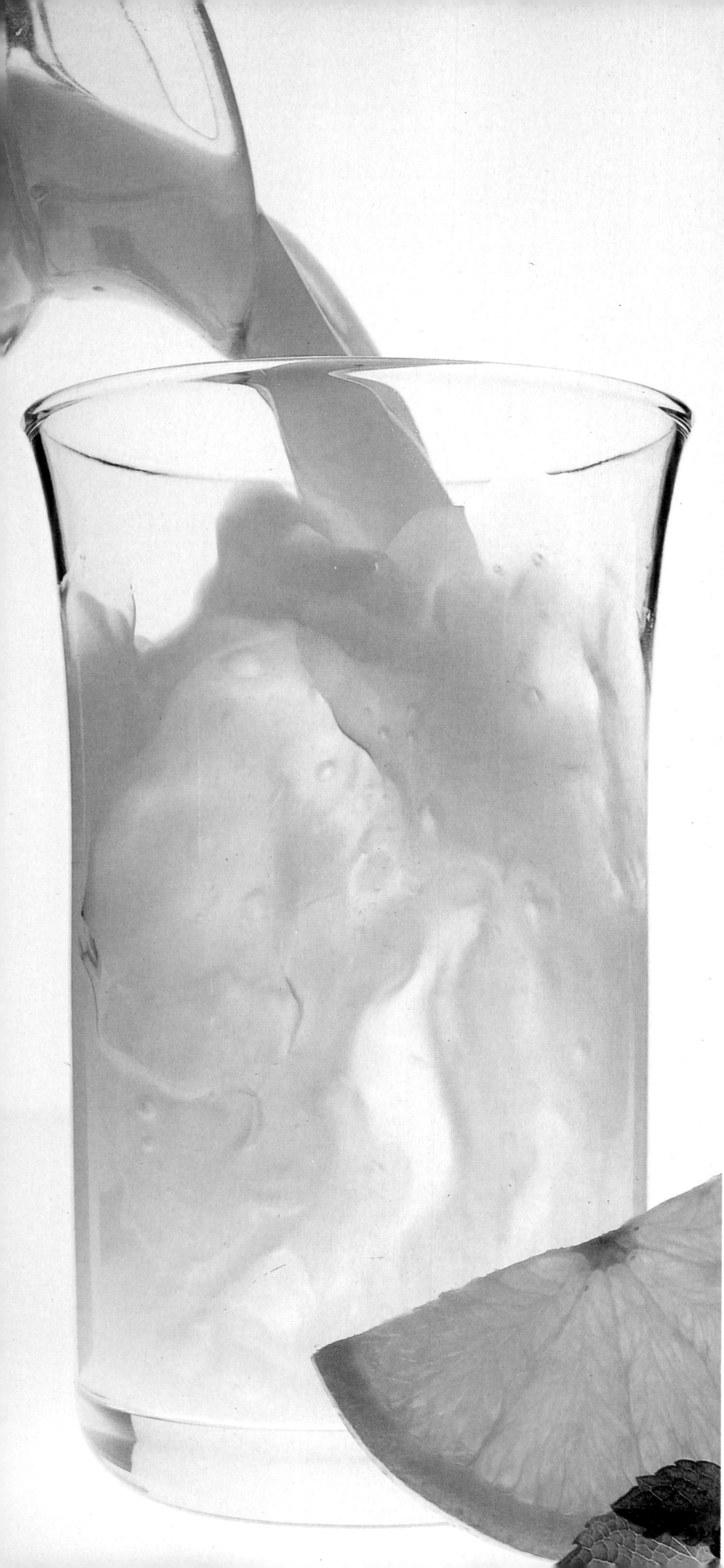

***Southern Country Brunch***
*6-8 servings*

*Pineapple-Orange Banana Cooler*
*Baked Eggs in Spinach Nests*
*Maple-glazed Ham Roll-ups*
*Pepper Cheese Grits*
*Assorted Sweet Rolls**
*Pink Lemonade*
*Dessert Squares*
*Cinnamon-spiced Coffee*

### Time Management

**The day before:** Prepare and refrigerate dessert.

**Early in the day:** Roll ham slices, place in plastic bag; chill. • Combine glaze ingredients. • Grate and chill cheese for grits. • Prepare juice cooler; chill. • Defrost hash browns and spinach. • Assemble "nest" mixture. Place in greased muffin cups and chill.

**About 1 hour before serving:** Heat conventional oven. • Bake spinach nests while microwaving grits. • Perk coffee and arrange rolls on serving platter.

**About 10 minutes before serving:** Arrange ham rolls in baking dish; microwave ham and glaze.

## Pineapple-Orange Banana Cooler

1 carton (64 oz.) pineapple-orange banana juice
1 quart club soda or carbonated lemon-lime soda
1 orange, halved and sliced

About 16 servings

In 3-quart pitcher, combine juice and club soda. Add orange slices, and stir to combine. Pour cooler into glasses.

| Per Serving: | |
|---|---|
| Calories: | 77 |
| Protein: | 1 g. |
| Carbohydrate: | 19 g. |
| Fat: | — |
| Sodium: | 2 mg. |
| Cholesterol: | — |

## Baked Eggs in Spinach Nests

1 pkg. (10 oz.) frozen chopped
  spinach
¼ cup margarine or butter,
  divided
3 cups frozen hash brown
  potato cubes, defrosted
14 eggs
1 tablespoon all-purpose flour
1 teaspoon finely chopped
  onion
½ teaspoon salt
¼ teaspoon white pepper
2 tablespoons half-and-half

6 to 8 servings

Heat conventional oven to 425°F. Generously grease twelve 3-inch muffin cups. Set aside. Unwrap spinach and place on plate. Microwave at High for 4 to 6 minutes, or until spinach is defrosted. Drain, pressing to remove excess moisture. Set aside. In small bowl, microwave 2 tablespoons margarine at High for 45 seconds to 1 minute, or until melted.

In large mixing bowl, combine spinach, margarine, hash browns, 2 eggs, flour, onion, salt and pepper. Mix well. Place heaping ¼ cup of spinach mixture in each prepared muffin cup. With back of tablespoon, press spinach mixture on bottom and up sides of each cup, forming ridge around top edge of each cup. Bake spinach nests for 22 to 25 minutes, or until edges are light brown. Remove from oven.

Reduce oven temperature to 350°F. Place 1 egg in each nest. Return to oven. Bake for 12 to 15 minutes, or until eggs are almost set. Remove from oven. Dot with remaining margarine. Place ½ teaspoon half-and-half on top of each egg. Return to oven. Bake for 5 to 7 minutes, or until eggs are set. Let stand for 1 minute. With narrow spatula, carefully remove each egg-filled nest and arrange on serving platter.

| Per Serving: | | | |
|---|---|---|---|
| Calories: | 253 | Fat: | 16 g. |
| Protein: | 13 g. | Sodium: | 358 mg. |
| Carbohydrate: | 13 g. | Cholesterol: | 482 mg. |

## Maple-glazed Ham Roll-ups

8 fully cooked ham slices (2 oz. each), about ¼ inch thick
½ cup maple syrup
1 tablespoon margarine or butter
½ teaspoon ground cinnamon

6 to 8 servings

Roll up each ham slice, jelly roll fashion. Secure with wooden picks. Arrange ham roll-ups in even layer in 10-inch square casserole. Cover. Microwave at High for 4 to 5 minutes, or until hot. Drain, if necessary. Re-cover to keep warm. Set aside. In 2-cup measure, combine remaining ingredients. Microwave at High for 1¾ to 2 minutes, or until margarine is melted and mixture begins to boil. Pour evenly over ham roll-ups. Serve with glaze spooned over ham.

Per Serving:
| | |
|---|---|
| Calories: | 145 |
| Protein: | 12 g. |
| Carbohydrate: | 14 g. |
| Fat: | 5 g. |
| Sodium: | 704 mg. |
| Cholesterol: | 30 mg. |

## Pepper Cheese Grits

2 cups hot water
¾ cup uncooked quick-cooking grits
¾ teaspoon salt
½ cup half-and-half
3 eggs
4 drops red pepper sauce
2 cups shredded hot pepper Monterey Jack cheese
¼ cup sliced green onions

6 to 8 servings

In 2-quart casserole, combine water, grits and salt. Cover. Microwave at High for 6 to 10 minutes, or until desired consistency, stirring twice. Set aside. In small mixing bowl, blend half-and-half, eggs and red pepper sauce. Add egg mixture, cheese and onions to cooked grits. Mix well. Re-cover. Microwave at 50% (Medium) for 10 to 15 minutes, or until mixture thickens and is hot, stirring twice. Garnish with cherry tomatoes and additional sliced green onion, if desired.

Per Serving:
| | | | |
|---|---|---|---|
| Calories: | 214 | Fat: | 13 g. |
| Protein: | 11 g. | Sodium: | 384 mg. |
| Carbohydrate: | 14 g. | Cholesterol: | 134 mg. |

## Cinnamon-spiced Coffee

½ cup regular grind coffee granules
3 cinnamon sticks
2 thin slices fresh nutmeg
20 cups water

About 16 servings

Place paper coffee filter in basket of 30-cup automatic coffee percolator. Add coffee granules, cinnamon sticks and nutmeg. Add water to percolator. Perk coffee for 25 to 30 minutes. Serve hot or iced.

Per Serving:
| | |
|---|---|
| Calories: | 2 |
| Protein: | — |
| Carbohydrate: | — |
| Fat: | — |
| Sodium: | 2 mg. |
| Cholesterol: | — |

## Pink Lemonade Dessert Squares

### Crust:
- ¾ cup margarine or butter, softened
- ⅓ cup powdered sugar
- 1 teaspoon grated lemon peel
- 1½ cups all-purpose flour

### Filling:
- 1 can (14 oz.) sweetened condensed milk
- 1 can (6 oz.) frozen pink lemonade
- 4 drops red food coloring
- 2¾ cups prepared whipped topping, divided
- 3 thin lemon slices, quartered

12 servings

Per Serving:
| | |
|---|---|
| Calories: | 361 |
| Protein: | 5 g. |
| Carbohydrate: | 46 g. |
| Fat: | 18 g. |
| Sodium: | 191 mg. |
| Cholesterol: | 14 mg. |

## How to Make Pink Lemonade Dessert Squares

**Heat** conventional oven to 350°F. Grease 13 × 9-inch baking pan. Set aside. In medium mixing bowl, beat margarine, powdered sugar and grated lemon peel at high speed of electric mixer, until light and fluffy. Add flour. Mix well. Pat dough evenly into prepared pan.

**Bake** for 18 to 20 minutes, or until light golden brown. Cool completely. In medium mixing bowl, place condensed milk, lemonade and food coloring. Beat at medium speed of electric mixer until blended. Fold in 2 cups prepared whipped topping.

**Pour** filling over cooled crust. Cover with plastic wrap. Chill at least 4 hours or overnight. Top each serving with dollop of remaining prepared whipped topping and 1 lemon slice quarter.

Spanish-style Pasta Salad
Parmesan-Romano Bread                    Strawberry Brownie Tart

### Time Management

**The day before:** Bake brownie tart base. • Prepare pasta salad; refrigerate in covered bowl. • Wash leaf lettuce; wrap in dampened paper towels and refrigerate in plastic bag.

**Early in the day:** Top brownie tart with strawberries; glaze and chill.

**About 15 to 30 minutes before serving:** Prepare bread; broil conventionally. • Line salad bowl with greens; top with salad.

## ◄ Spanish-style Pasta Salad

**Salad:**
1 pkg. (10 oz.) frozen tiny peas
1 pkg. (16 oz.) uncooked rosamarina (orzo) pasta
1½ lbs. bone-in whole chicken breasts (10 to 12 oz. each), split in half, skin removed
1 lb. large shrimp, shelled and deveined
1 medium green pepper, cut into thin strips
1 medium red pepper, cut into thin strips
10 jumbo pitted black olives, sliced
10 cherry tomatoes, quartered
1 jar (6½ oz.) marinated artichoke hearts, undrained

**Dressing:**
¼ cup olive oil
3 tablespoons fresh lemon juice
1½ teaspoons salt
¼ teaspoon pepper
⅛ to ¼ teaspoon ground saffron

8 servings

Rinse peas with cold water to defrost. Drain. Set aside. Prepare rosamarina as directed on package. Rinse and drain. Set aside.

Arrange chicken on roasting rack with thickest portions toward outside. Cover with wax paper. Microwave at High for 9½ to 11 minutes, or until chicken near bone is no longer pink and juices run clear, rearranging once or twice. Let stand, covered, for 3 minutes. Cool slightly. Remove meat from bones and cut into ¼ × 3-inch strips. Set aside.

Arrange shrimp in single layer in 10-inch square casserole. Cover. Microwave at 70% (Medium High) for 5 to 8 minutes, or until shrimp are opaque, stirring once. Let stand, covered, for 1 to 2 minutes. In large mixing bowl or salad bowl, combine peas, cooked rosamarina, chicken and shrimp. Add remaining salad ingredients. Toss gently to combine. In small mixing bowl, combine all dressing ingredients. Stir with whisk to blend. Pour over salad ingredients. Toss to coat. Cover. Chill 4 hours or overnight. Serve salad in lettuce-lined bowl, if desired.

Per Serving:
| | | | |
|---|---|---|---|
| Calories: | 471 | Fat: | 13 g. |
| Protein: | 33 g. | Sodium: | 627 mg. |
| Carbohydrate: | 53 g. | Cholesterol: | 105 mg. |

## ◄ Parmesan-Romano Bread

½ cup margarine or butter
¼ teaspoon white pepper
¼ cup grated Parmesan cheese
2 tablespoons grated Romano cheese
1 loaf (1 lb.) French bread, cut into 16 diagonal slices

8 servings

In small bowl, combine margarine and pepper. Microwave at High for 1½ to 1¾ minutes, or until margarine is melted. Set aside. In small mixing bowl, combine cheeses. Mix well. Set aside. Arrange bread slices in single layer on 15½ × 10½-inch jelly roll pan. Brush tops of slices with one-half of melted margarine mixture. Place slices under conventional broiler, 2 to 3 inches from heat. Broil until golden brown. Turn slices over; brush with remaining melted margarine. Sprinkle evenly with cheeses. Place under broiler. Continue to broil until golden brown. Serve warm.

Per Serving:
| | |
|---|---|
| Calories: | 287 |
| Protein: | 7 g. |
| Carbohydrate: | 32 g. |
| Fat: | 15 g. |
| Sodium: | 541 mg. |
| Cholesterol: | 6 mg. |

## Strawberry Brownie Tart

4 squares (1 oz. each)
    unsweetened chocolate
¼ cup margarine or butter
1 cup sugar
3 eggs
1 teaspoon vanilla
1 cup all-purpose flour
¼ cup milk
½ teaspoon baking powder
2 pkgs. (3 oz. each) cream
    cheese
¾ cup plus 2 tablespoons
    strawberry preserves,
    divided
4 drops red food coloring
1 quart fresh strawberries,
    sliced

12 servings

| Per Serving: | |
| --- | --- |
| Calories: | 339 |
| Protein: | 5 g. |
| Carbohydrate: | 47 g. |
| Fat: | 17 g. |
| Sodium: | 127 mg. |
| Cholesterol: | 85 mg. |

## How to Make Strawberry Brownie Tart

**Heat** conventional oven to 350°F. Grease bottom of 12-inch pizza pan. Set aside. In 2-cup measure, place chocolate and margarine. Microwave at 50% (Medium) for 3 to 5 minutes, or until mixture is melted and can be stirred smooth, stirring 2 or 3 times. Set aside.

**Combine** sugar, 2 eggs and vanilla in medium mixing bowl. Beat at high speed of electric mixer until well blended. Stir in melted chocolate mixture, the flour, milk and baking powder. Set aside.

**Microwave** cream cheese in small mixing bowl at 50% (Medium) for 1 to 1½ minutes, or until softened. Add remaining egg, 2 tablespoons strawberry preserves and the food coloring. Beat at medium speed of electric mixer until well blended. Set aside.

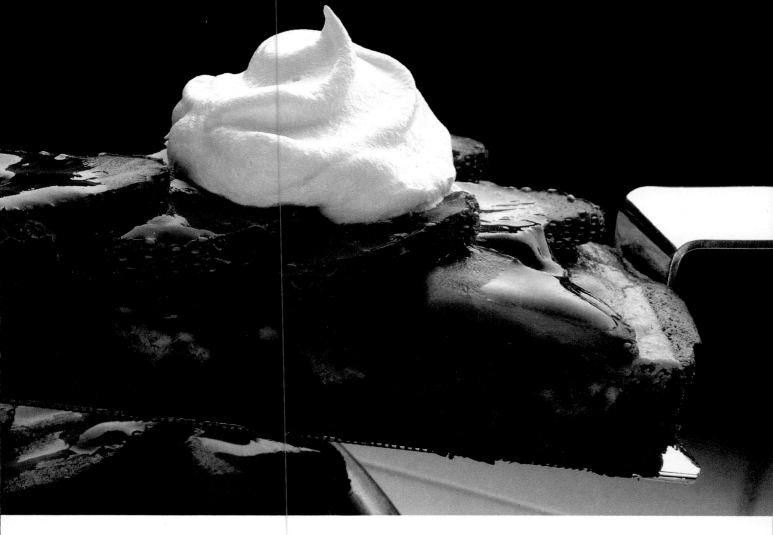

**Spread** one-half of brownie batter in prepared pan. Spread cream cheese mixture evenly over batter. Drop remaining batter by spoonfuls randomly over top. Swirl the two mixtures together with knife or spatula. Bake for 18 to 20 minutes, or until set. Cool completely.

**Arrange** strawberry slices in even layer on top of brownie. In 2-cup measure, place remaining ¾ cup strawberry preserves. Microwave at High for 1½ to 3 minutes, or until melted, stirring once.

**Strain** preserves. Discard pulp. Drizzle strained preserves over strawberries. Chill Strawberry Brownie Tart at least 2 hours, or until glaze is set. Serve topped with dollop of whipped cream, if desired.

## Cool Summer Evening
*6-8 servings*

### Florentine Chicken Breasts

Tri-colored Peppers      White Rice*      Cantaloupe Wedges*

Frozen Yogurt & Lime-Raspberry Sauce

### Time Management

**The day before:** Prepare Lime-Raspberry Sauce; cover and refrigerate. Mix spinach stuffing and stuff chicken breasts; cover and refrigerate. • Cut up peppers; refrigerate in plastic bag.

**About 1¼ hours before serving:** Heat conventional oven. • Bake chicken while you prepare rice and cut melon into wedges. • While chicken bakes for last 10 minutes, microwave peppers.

## Florentine Chicken Breasts

2  pkgs. (10 oz. each) frozen
      chopped spinach
1  pkg. (3 oz.) cream cheese
2  cups onion and garlic
      croutons, finely crushed
⅓  cup shredded carrot
2  tablespoons lemon juice
2  teaspoons dill seed
½  teaspoon salt
8  boneless whole chicken
      breasts (8 to 10 oz. each)

6 to 8 servings

Heat conventional oven to 375°F. Place spinach in 2-quart casserole. Microwave at High for 6 to 10 minutes, or until spinach is defrosted. Drain, pressing to remove excess moisture. Set aside.

In medium mixing bowl, microwave cream cheese at High for 15 to 30 seconds, or until softened. Add spinach, croutons, carrot, lemon juice, dill seed and salt. Mix well. Place ¼ cup packed spinach mixture in center of each chicken breast. Fold all sides of chicken over spinach mixture. Secure with wooden picks. Place breasts in 13 × 9-inch baking dish. Bake for 1 hour to 1 hour 10 minutes, or until chicken is golden brown, basting with drippings 2 or 3 times.

Per Serving:
Calories:                   472
Protein:                    74 g.
Carbohydrate:            9 g.
Fat:                         13 g.
Sodium:                    509 mg.
Cholesterol:              204 mg.

## Tri-colored Peppers

2  medium green peppers, cut
      into thin strips
1  medium red pepper, cut into
      thin strips
1  medium yellow pepper, cut
      into thin strips

2  tablespoons olive oil
2  teaspoons red wine vinegar
1½  teaspoons sugar
¼  teaspoon salt

6 to 8 servings

In 2-quart casserole, combine peppers. In 1-cup measure, combine remaining ingredients. Mix well. Add vinegar mixture to peppers. Toss to coat. Cover. Microwave at High for 6 to 10 minutes, or until peppers are tender, stirring once.

Per Serving:
Calories:              48        Fat:                    4 g.
Protein:               1 g.      Sodium:             69 mg.
Carbohydrate:      4 g.      Cholesterol:        —

## Frozen Yogurt & Lime-Raspberry Sauce

1  pkg. (10 oz.) frozen
      raspberries in light syrup
¼  cup lime juice

1  tablespoon powdered sugar
2  teaspoons cornstarch
2  pints frozen raspberry yogurt

16 servings

Flex frozen raspberry pouch to break up fruit. With knife, cut large "X" in pouch. Place, cut-side-down, in 1-quart casserole. Microwave at High for 2 to 3 minutes, or until outer fruit feels slightly warm. Lift corners of pouch to release fruit into casserole. Stir. Let stand for 5 minutes. Place raspberries in food processor or blender. Process until smooth. Strain raspberries into 4-cup measure. Discard seeds. Add lime juice, powdered sugar and cornstarch to raspberry liquid. Mix well. Microwave at High for 3 to 5 minutes, or until sauce is thickened and translucent, stirring twice. Cover and chill. Serve Lime-Raspberry Sauce over frozen yogurt.

Per Serving:
Calories:              72        Fat:                    2 g.
Protein:               1 g.      Sodium:             31 mg.
Carbohydrate:      12 g.     Cholesterol:        3 mg.

## Broiled Lime-basted Swordfish

2 to 2½ lbs. swordfish steaks,
    about 1 inch thick, cut into
    serving-size pieces
3 tablespoons butter
2 tablespoons white wine
1 tablespoon lime juice
1 teaspoon grated lime peel
¼ teaspoon sugar
¼ teaspoon salt

6 to 8 servings

Arrange swordfish steaks on conventional broiler pan. Set aside. In 2-cup measure, combine remaining ingredients. Microwave at High for 1¼ to 2 minutes, or until butter is melted. Stir to combine. Brush swordfish steaks with one-half of mixture. Place swordfish steaks under conventional broiler, 4 to 5 inches from heat. Broil for about 10 to 14 minutes, or until fish flakes easily with fork, turning steaks over and basting once with remaining butter mixture.

Per Serving:

| | | | |
|---|---|---|---|
| Calories: | 166 | Fat: | 8 g. |
| Protein: | 20 g. | Sodium: | 209 mg. |
| Carbohydrate: | 1 g. | Cholesterol: | 40 mg. |

## Portuguese Rice

| | |
|---|---|
| 3 cups hot water | 1 tablespoon snipped fresh |
| 1½ cups uncooked long-grain | parsley |
| white rice | 1 teaspoon salt |
| ⅓ cup chopped red pepper | 1 teaspoon instant chicken |
| ¼ cup sliced green onions | bouillon granules |
| 6 extra-large pitted black | ¼ teaspoon ground turmeric |
| olives, cut into slivers | |

6 to 8 servings

In 3-quart casserole, combine all ingredients. Cover. Microwave at High for 8 minutes. Microwave at 50% (Medium) for 15 to 28 minutes longer, or until rice is tender and liquid is absorbed. Let stand, covered, for 5 minutes. Before serving, fluff with fork.

Per Serving:
| | | | |
|---|---|---|---|
| Calories: | 134 | Fat: | 1 g. |
| Protein: | 3 g. | Sodium: | 340 mg. |
| Carbohydrate: | 29 g. | Cholesterol: | — |

## Zucchini Strips with Cilantro Butter

| | |
|---|---|
| 2 medium zucchini, cut into | ½ teaspoon dried cilantro |
| julienne strips (2 × ¼-inch) | leaves |
| 2 tablespoons margarine or | ¼ teaspoon crushed red |
| butter | pepper flakes |
| | ¼ teaspoon salt |

6 to 8 servings

In 2-quart casserole, combine all ingredients. Cover. Microwave at High for 7 to 9 minutes, or until zucchini is tender, stirring once or twice.

Per Serving.
| | | | |
|---|---|---|---|
| Calories: | 30 | Fat: | 3 g. |
| Protein: | — | Sodium: | 101 mg. |
| Carbohydrate: | 1 g. | Cholesterol: | — |

## ◄ Rainbow Ice Cream Terrine

| | |
|---|---|
| ⅔ cup hot fudge topping | |
| 1 pint raspberry sherbet | |
| 1 pint orange sherbet | |
| 1 cup mixed nuts, chopped | |
| 1 pint chocolate ice cream | |

12 servings

Cut 16 × 8¼-inch piece of wax paper. Place wax paper in 9 × 5-inch loaf pan, leaving 3-inch overhang on each side. Place lined pan in freezer for at least 30 minutes. In 4-cup measure, microwave hot fudge topping at High for 45 seconds to 1 minute, or until topping can be stirred smooth. Set aside.

Remove covers from sherbets. Microwave 1 pint of sherbet at 50% (Medium) for 30 seconds to 1 minute, or until softened. Repeat with remaining pint of sherbet. Spread softened raspberry sherbet evenly in bottom of prepared loaf pan. Sprinkle evenly with nuts. Spread softened orange sherbet over nuts. Pour and spread hot fudge topping evenly over orange sherbet. Freeze terrine for 20 minutes, or until slightly set.

Remove cover from ice cream. Microwave at 50% (Medium) for 30 seconds to 1 minute, or until softened. Spread softened ice cream over hot fudge layer. Freeze at least 8 hours or overnight. To serve, loosen edges with spatula. Invert on serving platter. Remove wax paper. Serve in slices.

Per Serving:
| | |
|---|---|
| Calories: | 248 |
| Protein: | 4 g. |
| Carbohydrate: | 36 g. |
| Fat: | 11 g. |
| Sodium: | 65 mg. |
| Cholesterol: | 15 mg. |

### *Cajun Fish Fry*
*6-8 servings*

*Cajun Fried Fish Fillets*
*Dirty Rice*
*Mixed Salad of Boston &*
*Red Leaf Lettuce with*
*Oil & Vinegar Dressing**
*Upside-down*
*Peach Praline Pie*

#### Time Management

**The day before:** Prepare, cool and cover pie. • Cut up and refrigerate vegetables for rice. • Wash salad greens; refrigerate. • Mix pecan coating for fish.

**About 45 minutes before serving:** Start microwaving rice. • After you reduce power for rice, coat fish fillets and fry conventionally. • While rice stands, keep fish warm and toss salad.

## Cajun Fried Fish Fillets

2 eggs, lightly beaten
2 tablespoons milk

**Coating:**
1 cup finely chopped pecans
⅔ cup unseasoned dry bread crumbs
1 teaspoon salt
½ teaspoon cayenne
¼ teaspoon freshly ground pepper
½ cup all-purpose flour

2 lbs. sole fillets, about ¼ to ½ inch thick, cut into serving-size pieces
¼ cup margarine or butter, divided
¼ cup vegetable oil, divided

6 to 8 servings

In 9-inch pie plate, blend eggs and milk. Set aside. Mix all coating ingredients, except flour, on sheet of wax paper. Place flour on another sheet of wax paper. Pat sole fillets dry and dredge each piece in flour. Dip each fillet in egg mixture, then in crumb mixture, pressing lightly to coat both sides. In 12-inch skillet, heat 2 tablespoons margarine and 2 tablespoons oil conventionally over medium heat. Fry one-half of the fillets until golden brown, 6 to 8 minutes, turning once. Repeat with remaining margarine, oil and fillets.

| Per Serving: | | | |
|---|---|---|---|
| Calories: | 396 | Fat: | 26 g. |
| Protein: | 26 g. | Sodium: | 506 mg. |
| Carbohydrate: | 15 g. | Cholesterol: | 124 mg. |

# Dirty Rice

¾ lb. bulk pork sausage
1 cup chopped celery
1 cup coarsely chopped red or green pepper
½ cup chopped onion
1 clove garlic, minced
3 cups hot water
1½ cups long-grain white rice
2 teaspoons instant chicken bouillon granules
¾ to 1 teaspoon cayenne
¾ teaspoon freshly ground pepper
½ teaspoon ground cumin
½ teaspoon dried thyme leaves
½ teaspoon salt

6 to 8 servings

In 3-quart casserole, combine sausage, celery, red pepper, onion and garlic. Mix well. Cover. Microwave at High for 8 to 10 minutes, or until meat is no longer pink, stirring once to break apart. Drain. Add remaining ingredients. Mix well. Re-cover. Microwave at High for 5 minutes. Stir. Re-cover. Microwave at 50% (Medium) for 23 to 25 minutes, or until rice is tender and liquid is absorbed. Let stand, covered, for 5 minutes. Before serving, fluff with fork.

Per Serving:
| | | | |
|---|---|---|---|
| Calories: | 214 | Fat: | 7 g. |
| Protein: | 7 g. | Sodium: | 504 mg. |
| Carbohydrate: | 31 g. | Cholesterol: | 17 mg. |

## Upside-down Peach Praline Pie

| | |
|---|---|
| 4 cups water | 2¼ cups all-purpose flour |
| 6 medium peaches | ½ teaspoon salt |
| 1 cup packed brown sugar, divided | ¾ cup shortening |
| ¼ cup cornstarch | 5 to 6 tablespoons ice water |
| 2 tablespoons lemon juice | ½ cup pecan halves |
| ½ teaspoon ground cinnamon | ¼ cup margarine or butter |
| | 1 tablespoon light corn syrup |

8 servings

Heat conventional oven to 375°F. Place water in 2-quart casserole. Cover. Microwave at High for 8 to 11 minutes, or until water boils. Place 3 peaches in water. Let stand for 1 to 1½ minutes, to loosen skin. Repeat with remaining peaches. Immerse peaches in cold water. Peel and slice peaches. Place peach slices in medium mixing bowl. Add ½ cup brown sugar, the cornstarch, lemon juice and cinnamon. Toss gently to coat. Set aside. Continue as directed, right.

| Per Serving: | | | |
|---|---|---|---|
| Calories: | 548 | Fat: | 30 g. |
| Protein: | 5 g. | Sodium: | 214 mg. |
| Carbohydrate: | 68 g. | Cholesterol: | — |

## How to Make Upside-down Peach Praline Pie

**Combine** flour and salt in small mixing bowl. Cut in shortening to form coarse crumbs. Sprinkle with water, 1 tablespoon at a time, mixing with fork until particles are moistened and cling together.

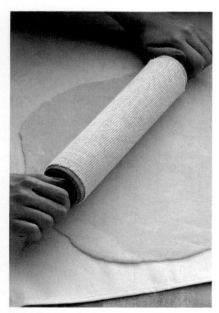

**Form** dough into 2 equal-size balls. Roll out 1 ball of dough on lightly floured board, at least 2 inches larger than inverted 9-inch pie plate. Ease into plate. Spoon peach filling into pie crust. Roll out remaining dough. Place top crust over peach filling.

**Trim** and flute edges. Cut several vents in top crust. Bake for 50 minutes to 1 hour, or until crust is golden brown. Cool pie upright in pan for 5 minutes. Invert onto serving plate. Decorate with pecan halves.

**Combine** remaining ½ cup brown sugar, the margarine and corn syrup in 4-cup measure. Microwave at High for 1 to 2¼ minutes, or until mixture begins to boil, stirring once. Boil for 1 minute. Pour evenly over pecan halves. Let cool at least 1 hour before serving.

<br>

## Old-fashioned Sunday Supper
*6-8 servings*

Oven-baked Rump Roast with Gravy
Oven-browned Potatoes     Bean & Carrot Amandine
Frozen Fruit Salad     Glazed Apple Spice Cake

### Time Management

**The day before, or early in the day:** Prepare and freeze salad. • Prepare dessert. Cool and cover.

**About 2 to 2½ hours before serving:** Heat conventional oven and prepare roast for cooking. • While roast bakes, prepare potatoes; place in oven 1½ hours before roast is done. • During last 20 minutes of baking time, microwave vegetables. • While roast stands, strain drippings and microwave gravy.

## Oven-baked Rump Roast

| | |
|---|---|
| 3 to 5-lb. beef rump roast | ¼ teaspoon salt |
| 1 can (6 oz.) vegetable juice cocktail | ¼ teaspoon pepper |
| ½ cup water | 4 medium carrots, cut into 1-inch lengths (about 2 cups) |
| 2 tablespoons packed brown sugar | 3 medium ribs of celery, cut into 1-inch lengths (about 1 cup) |
| 1 tablespoon Worcestershire sauce | 1 medium onion, cut into eighths |

6 to 8 servings

Heat conventional oven to 350°F. Place roast in nylon cooking bag. Place bag in 13 × 9-inch baking dish. Set aside. In 2-cup measure, combine vegetable juice cocktail, water, brown sugar, Worcestershire sauce, salt and pepper. Pour over roast. Add vegetables to bag. Secure bag with nylon tie or string. Estimate total cooking time at 25 to 30 minutes per pound. Bake until beef is tender. Reserve drippings for gravy (below).

Per Serving:

| | | | |
|---|---|---|---|
| Calories: | 275 | Fat: | 9 g. |
| Protein: | 38 g. | Sodium: | 279 mg. |
| Carbohydrate: | 9 g. | Cholesterol: | 88 mg. |

## Gravy

| | |
|---|---|
| 1 cup reserved drippings | ⅛ teaspoon salt |
| ½ cup water | ⅛ teaspoon pepper |
| 3 tablespoons all-purpose flour | |

About 1½ cups

Strain drippings into 4-cup measure. Add water. In small mixing bowl, place remaining ingredients. Add small amount of drippings to flour mixture. Stir until mixture is smooth. Add back to remaining drippings, stirring with whisk until smooth. Microwave at High for 3 to 6 minutes, or until mixture thickens and bubbles, stirring twice.

Per Serving:

| | | | |
|---|---|---|---|
| Calories: | 72 | Fat: | 7 g. |
| Protein: | — | Sodium: | 34 mg. |
| Carbohydrate: | 2 g. | Cholesterol: | 7 mg. |

## Oven-browned Potatoes

| |
|---|
| 3 tablespoons margarine or butter |
| ¾ teaspoon seasoned salt |
| ¼ teaspoon pepper |
| 3 cans (16 oz. each) small whole potatoes, drained |

6 to 8 servings

Heat conventional oven to 350°F. In small mixing bowl, microwave margarine at High for 1 to 1¼ minutes, or until melted. Add salt and pepper. Mix well. Roll each potato in margarine mixture. Arrange potatoes in single layer in 13 × 9-inch baking dish. Bake for 1 hour 15 minutes to 1 hour 30 minutes, or until golden brown, turning potatoes over once.

Per Serving:

| | |
|---|---|
| Calories: | 102 |
| Protein: | 2 g. |
| Carbohydrate: | 15 g. |
| Fat: | 5 g. |
| Sodium: | 476 mg. |
| Cholesterol: | — |

## Bean & Carrot Amandine

| |
|---|
| 2 pkgs. (10 oz. each) frozen French-cut green beans |
| 1 cup shredded carrots |
| ⅓ cup sliced almonds |
| 2 tablespoons margarine or butter |

6 to 8 servings

In 2-quart casserole, place beans and carrots. Cover. Microwave at High for 12 to 15 minutes, or until hot, stirring 3 or 4 times. Drain. Recover. Set aside. In 9-inch pie plate, place almonds and margarine. Microwave at High for 4 to 6 minutes, or until almonds are golden brown, stirring twice. Sprinkle almonds over beans and carrots. Toss to combine.

Per Serving:

| | |
|---|---|
| Calories: | 72 |
| Protein: | 2 g. |
| Carbohydrate: | 6 g. |
| Fat: | 5 g. |
| Sodium: | 47 mg. |
| Cholesterol: | — |

## Frozen Fruit Salad

- 4 oz. cream cheese
- 1 tablespoon mayonnaise
- 1 tablespoon sugar
- 1 pkg. (10 oz.) frozen strawberries in syrup
- 1 can (20 oz.) pineapple tidbits, drained
- 2 medium bananas, cut in half lengthwise and sliced
- 1 cup prepared whipped topping
- ½ cup chopped walnuts
- 16 small fresh strawberries

8 to 16 servings

Place 16 foil baking cups on baking sheet. Set aside. In medium mixing bowl, microwave cream cheese at High for 30 to 45 seconds, or until softened. Add mayonnaise and sugar. Mix well. Stir in frozen strawberries, pineapple, bananas, whipped topping and walnuts. Spoon ⅓ cup fruit salad mixture into each baking cup. Cut each fresh strawberry lengthwise into thin slices, almost to stem. Fan each strawberry slightly. Garnish each serving with one strawberry fan. Place fruit salads in freezer. Freeze at least 2 hours or overnight. Place frozen salads in large plastic food-storage bags. Seal. Freeze salads up to 2 months. Before serving, let salads stand at room temperature for 10 minutes.

Per Serving:
| | |
|---|---|
| Calories: | 115 |
| Protein: | 2 g. |
| Carbohydrate: | 15 g. |
| Fat: | 6 g. |
| Sodium: | 31 mg. |
| Cholesterol: | 9 mg. |

## Glazed Apple Spice Cake

⅓ cup margarine or butter
¾ cup sugar
1 cup applesauce
1 egg
2¼ cups all-purpose flour
2 teaspoons baking soda
1 teaspoon ground cinnamon
½ teaspoon freshly grated nutmeg
¼ teaspoon ground cloves
¼ teaspoon salt
2 cups thin McIntosh apple slices
¼ cup red currant jelly
Prepared whipped topping

12 servings

Heat conventional oven to 350°F. Grease 9-inch springform pan. Set aside. In large mixing bowl, combine margarine and sugar. Beat at medium speed of electric mixer until light and fluffy. Add applesauce and egg. Mix well. Add remaining ingredients, except apples, jelly and whipped topping. Beat at low speed of electric mixer for 1 minute, or until moistened, scraping bowl occasionally.

Spread batter evenly in prepared pan. Arrange apple slices, skin-side-up, in circular pattern around edges of cake, placing 8 slices in center. Press slices gently into batter. Bake for 1 hour to 1 hour 10 minutes, or until wooden pick inserted in center comes out clean. Place on cooling rack. In 1-cup measure, microwave currant jelly at High for 45 seconds to 1 minute, or until jelly is melted and can be stirred smooth. Brush jelly evenly over top of cake. Cool 20 minutes. Loosen edges with spatula and remove sides of pan. Serve in wedges. Garnish with whipped topping.

| Per Serving: | | | |
|---|---|---|---|
| Calories: | 251 | Fat: | 8 g. |
| Protein: | 3 g. | Sodium: | 256 mg. |
| Carbohydrate: | 42 g. | Cholesterol: | 24 mg. |

## White Cheddar Dip

4 cups shredded white Cheddar cheese
2 tablespoons all-purpose flour
¼ teaspoon dry mustard
¼ teaspoon onion powder
¾ cup half-and-half
½ teaspoon Worcestershire sauce
1 loaf (1 lb.) unsliced pumpernickel bread
  Paprika
  Red and green apple slices

8 servings

In 8-cup measure, combine cheese, flour, dry mustard and onion powder. Toss to coat. Stir in half-and-half and Worcestershire sauce. Microwave at 50% (Medium) for 5 to 7 minutes, or until mixture can be stirred smooth, stirring twice with whisk. Set aside. Cut 1 to 1½-inch slice from top of bread. Cut around inside of loaf, leaving ½ inch of bread around outside. Remove center, leaving at least 1 inch of bread on bottom. Cut center and top into pieces for dipping. Spoon warm cheese mixture into bread shell. Sprinkle with paprika. Serve with bread cubes and apple slices for dippers.

| Per Serving: | | | |
|---|---|---|---|
| Calories: | 405 | Fat: | 22 g. |
| Protein: | 20 g. | Sodium: | 686 mg. |
| Carbohydrate: | 33 g. | Cholesterol: | 68 mg. |

## Hearthside Beef Stew

2-lb. boneless beef top round
    steak, about 1 inch thick, cut
    into 1-inch pieces
⅓  cup all-purpose flour
1  can (28 oz.) Italian plum-style
    whole tomatoes, cut up and
    undrained
2  cups thinly sliced carrots
½  cup coarsely chopped onion
1  teaspoon ground cumin
½  teaspoon ground cinnamon
½  teaspoon salt
½  teaspoon sugar
¼  teaspoon garlic powder
¼  teaspoon cayenne
2  cups coarsely chopped red
    peppers

8 servings

In 3-quart casserole, combine
meat and flour. Toss to coat. Add
remaining ingredients, except red
peppers. Cover. Microwave at
High for 10 minutes. Stir. Re-cover.
Microwave at 50% (Medium) for
45 minutes to 1 hour, or until meat
is tender, stirring twice. Stir in peppers. Re-cover. Microwave at 50%
(Medium) for 10 to 15 minutes, or
until peppers are tender-crisp. Let
stand, covered, for 5 minutes.

Per Serving:
Calories:    233
Protein:    29 g.
Carbohydrate:    15 g.
Fat:    6 g.
Sodium:    362 mg.
Cholesterol:    71 mg.

## Parsleyed Couscous

3  cups hot water
¼  cup margarine or butter
½  teaspoon salt
⅛  teaspoon cayenne
2  cups uncooked couscous
½  cup snipped fresh parsley

8 servings

In 2-quart casserole, combine water, margarine, salt and cayenne.
Cover. Microwave at High for 5½ to 7 minutes, or until boiling. Stir in
couscous. Re-cover. Let stand for 5 minutes. Stir in parsley. Before
serving, fluff couscous lightly with fork.

Per Serving:
Calories:    163    Fat:    6 g.
Protein:    4 g.    Sodium:    204 mg.
Carbohydrate:    23 g.    Cholesterol:    —

## Apple Crunch Salad

⅓ cup creamy peanut butter
2 tablespoons mayonnaise
1 tablespoon honey
1 teaspoon lemon juice
⅛ teaspoon ground cinnamon
    Dash ground cloves
3 cups cored unpeeled
    chopped Granny Smith
    apples
1 cup dry-roasted peanuts
1 cup chopped dates
½ cup golden raisins
½ cup shredded carrot

8 servings

In small mixing bowl, combine peanut butter, mayonnaise, honey, lemon juice, cinnamon and cloves. Mix well. Set aside. In large mixing bowl or salad bowl, combine remaining ingredients. Add peanut butter mixture. Toss to coat. Cover and chill for 1 to 2 hours before serving.

Per Serving:
| | |
|---|---|
| Calories: | 318 |
| Protein: | 9 g. |
| Carbohydrate: | 38 g. |
| Fat: | 17 g. |
| Sodium: | 77 mg. |
| Cholesterol: | 2 mg. |

# Lemon Pudding Cake

### Cake:

- 3 tablespoons margarine or butter
- 4 eggs, separated
- 1 cup sugar
- ¾ cup all-purpose flour
- ¼ teaspoon ground coriander
- 1 teaspoon grated orange peel
- 1 teaspoon grated lemon peel
- 1½ cups milk
- ⅓ cup orange juice
- ¼ cup lemon juice

### Sauce:

- ½ cup margarine or butter
- 1 cup powdered sugar
- ¼ cup half-and-half
- 2 teaspoons lemon juice
- ¼ teaspoon grated orange peel
- ¼ teaspoon grated lemon peel

8 to 10 servings

Heat conventional oven to 325°F. In small bowl, microwave 3 tablespoons margarine at High for 1 to 1¼ minutes, or until melted. Set aside. In medium mixing bowl, beat egg whites at high speed of electric mixer until stiff but not dry. Set aside.

In large mixing bowl, beat egg yolks slightly. Add remaining cake ingredients except melted margarine and egg whites. Beat at medium speed of electric mixer until smooth. Beat in melted margarine. Fold in egg whites. Pour mixture into 10-inch square casserole. Bake for 40 to 45 minutes, or until top is golden brown and firm to the touch. Cool for 5 minutes before serving.

In 4-cup measure, microwave ½ cup margarine at High for 1½ to 1¾ minutes, or until melted. Stir in remaining sauce ingredients. Microwave at 50% (Medium) for 1 to 2 minutes, or until smooth, stirring once. Serve warm sauce over pudding cake.

| Per Serving: | | | |
|---|---|---|---|
| Calories: | 326 | Fat: | 16 g. |
| Protein: | 5 g. | Sodium: | 197 mg. |
| Carbohydrate: | 41 g. | Cholesterol: | 115 mg. |

### *Fall Is in the Air*
*6-8 servings*

*Brandy Peppered Pork Chops*
*Lemony Risotto*
*Homegrown Tomato & Cucumber Salad*
*Mixed Fall Fruit Crisp*

## Time Management

**About 1¾ hours before serving:** Prepare fruit crisp.

**About 1 hour before serving:** Brown chops and prepare for baking while conventional oven heats. • While chops bake, microwave risotto; slice tomatoes and cucumbers. • Microwave sauce while chops and risotto stand.

# ◄ Brandy Peppered Pork Chops

1 teaspoon freshly ground
   pepper
8 pork chops (8 oz. each),
   about 1 inch thick
1 tablespoon margarine or
   butter
½ cup cranberry-apple juice
⅓ cup brandy
¼ cup chopped onion

**Sauce:**

2 tablespoons cranberry-apple
   juice
1 tablespoon cornstarch
1 cup reserved pan drippings
¼ teaspoon salt
1 tablespoon snipped fresh
   parsley

6 to 8 servings

Heat conventional oven to 350°F. Sprinkle pepper evenly on both sides of pork chops. Set aside. In 10-inch skillet, melt margarine conventionally over medium-high heat. Brown four chops on both sides over medium-high heat, about 3 to 5 minutes on each side. Repeat with remaining chops. Arrange browned chops slightly overlapping in 13 × 9-inch baking dish. Set aside.

Drain and discard drippings from skillet. To same skillet, add ½ cup cranberry-apple juice and the brandy. Bring mixture to a boil. Simmer over medium heat for 5 minutes. Pour mixture evenly over pork chops in baking dish. Sprinkle chops with onion. Cover baking dish with foil. Bake chops for 40 to 50 minutes, or until meat is tender and no longer pink. Remove chops from drippings and arrange on serving platter. Reserve drippings. Cover chops to keep warm. Set aside.

In small bowl, mix 2 tablespoons cranberry-apple juice with cornstarch. Stir to dissolve. Place reserved drippings in 4-cup measure. Add cornstarch mixture and salt. Stir. Microwave at High for 2½ to 3 minutes, or until sauce is thickened and translucent, stirring every minute. Pour sauce over chops. Sprinkle with parsley.

Per Serving:

| | | | | |
|---|---|---|---|---|
| Calories: | 377 | Fat: | 20 g. |
| Protein: | 36 g. | Sodium: | 173 mg. |
| Carbohydrate: | 4 g. | Cholesterol: | 117 mg. |

# ◄ Lemony Risotto

1 cup arborio rice
¼ cup chopped onion
2 tablespoons olive oil
1 tablespoon margarine or
   butter
3 cups hot water
1½ teaspoons grated lemon
   peel
1 tablespoon fresh lemon
   juice
1½ teaspoons instant chicken
   bouillon granules
1 cup frozen peas
¼ cup grated Parmesan
   cheese
1 tablespoon snipped fresh
   parsley

6 to 8 servings

In 2-quart casserole, combine rice, onion, olive oil and margarine. Microwave at High for 5 to 6 minutes, or until rice just begins to turn light golden brown, stirring every two minutes. Stir in water, lemon peel, lemon juice and chicken bouillon. Microwave, uncovered, at High for 18 to 23 minutes, or until rice is creamy and most liquid is absorbed, stirring every 5 minutes. Set aside. Place peas in 1-quart casserole. Microwave at High for 2 to 3 minutes, or until defrosted, stirring once to break apart. Add peas, cheese and parsley to rice mixture. Mix well. Cover. Microwave at High for 1 to 2 minutes, our until hot.

Per Serving:

| | | | | |
|---|---|---|---|---|
| Calories: | 158 | Fat: | 6 g. |
| Protein: | 4 g. | Sodium: | 166 mg. |
| Carbohydrate: | 22 g. | Cholesterol: | 3 mg. |

## Homegrown Tomato & Cucumber Salad

2 medium tomatoes, sliced
   (¼-inch slices)
1 medium cucumber, sliced
   (¼-inch slices)
2 tablespoons vegetable oil
1 tablespoon red wine vinegar
⅛ teaspoon garlic salt
⅛ teaspoon freshly ground
   pepper
1 tablespoon snipped fresh
   parsley

6 servings

Arrange tomato and cucumber slices on serving platter. Set aside. In small bowl, combine remaining ingredients, except parsley. Drizzle over tomato and cucumber slices. Sprinkle with parsley. Cover and chill at least 1 hour.

| Per Serving: | | | |
|---|---|---|---|
| Calories: | 51 | Fat: | 5 g. |
| Protein: | — | Sodium: | 41 mg. |
| Carbohydrate: | 3 g. | Cholesterol: | — |

## Mixed Fall Fruit Crisp

**Topping:**

¾ cup old-fashioned rolled oats
⅓ cup packed brown sugar
⅓ cup all-purpose flour
¼ cup chopped walnuts
½ teaspoon pumpkin pie spice
¼ cup margarine or butter

**Filling:**

1 pkg. (8 oz.) mixed dried fruits
2 medium Red Delicious pears,
   cored and sliced
2 medium red Rome apples,
   cored and sliced
½ cup cranberry juice
⅓ cup packed brown sugar
1 tablespoon cornstarch
1 teaspoon pumpkin pie spice

6 to 8 servings

Heat conventional oven to 375°F. In medium mixing bowl, combine all topping ingredients except margarine. Cut in margarine. Spread topping mixture in even layer on baking sheet. Bake for 10 to 12 minutes, or until golden brown, stirring mixture twice. Set aside to cool.

In 2-quart casserole, combine all filling ingredients. Mix well. Cover. Microwave at High for 13 to 17 minutes, or until fruit is tender and sauce is thickened and translucent, stirring twice. Sprinkle with topping. Microwave at High, uncovered, for 2 to 3 minutes, or until hot and bubbly around edges. Serve topped with vanilla or cinnamon ice cream, if desired.

| Per Serving: | | | |
|---|---|---|---|
| Calories: | 311 | Fat: | 9 g. |
| Protein: | 3 g. | Sodium: | 79 mg. |
| Carbohydrate: | 58 g. | Cholesterol: | — |

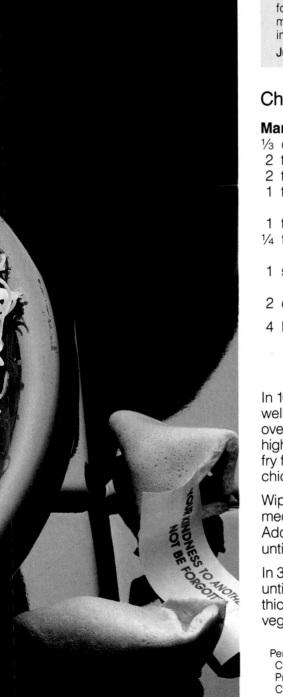

*Chicken & Walnut Stir-fry*
*Chinese Rice Noodles or Vermicelli**
*Orange & Lemon Sherbet**      *Fortune Cookies**

### Time Management

**The day before:** Cut up and marinate chicken. • Slice carrots and onions. Place in plastic bags with dampened paper towels; refrigerate. • Wash and tear spinach; wrap in dampened paper towels; refrigerate.

**About 30 minutes before serving:** Combine cornstarch and broth. • Heat water for noodles and stir-fry chicken and vegetables conventionally while you microwave sauce. • Boil noodles while microwaving chicken and vegetables in sauce.

**Just before serving:** Scoop sherbet into dessert dishes; garnish with mint leaves.

## Chicken & Walnut Stir-fry

### Marinade:

⅓ cup soy sauce
2 tablespoons vegetable oil
2 tablespoons dry sherry
1 tablespoon plus 1½ teaspoons cornstarch
1 tablespoon sugar
¼ teaspoon freshly ground pepper
1 small onion, cut in half and thinly sliced
2 cloves garlic, minced

4 boneless whole chicken breasts (8 to 10 oz. each), skin removed, cut into 1-inch pieces

### Vegetable Mixture:

¼ cup water
2 cups diagonally sliced carrots, ¼-inch slices
¾ cup diagonally sliced green onions
⅔ cup walnut halves
1 lb. fresh spinach, trimmed and torn into bite-size pieces

### Sauce:

1 can (14½ oz.) ready-to-serve chicken broth
2 tablespoons cornstarch

6 to 8 servings

In 10-inch square casserole, combine all marinade ingredients. Mix well. Add chicken pieces. Toss to coat. Cover and chill 45 minutes or overnight. Heat 12-inch nonstick skillet conventionally over medium-high heat. Add one-third of chicken pieces and marinade mixture. Stir-fry for 3 to 4 minutes, or until golden brown. Repeat with remaining chicken. Set aside.

Wipe out skillet with paper towels. Add water and carrots. Stir-fry over medium-high heat for 2 to 3 minutes, or until carrots are tender-crisp. Add onions and walnuts; continue stir-frying for 1½ to 2 minutes, or until onion is tender-crisp. Remove from heat; add spinach. Set aside.

In 3-quart casserole, combine broth and cornstarch. Stir with whisk until smooth. Microwave at High for 9 to 11 minutes, or until sauce is thickened and translucent, stirring every 2 minutes. Stir in chicken and vegetables. Cover. Microwave at High for 3 minutes, or until hot.

| Per Serving: | | | |
|---|---|---|---|
| Calories: | 306 | Fat: | 13 g. |
| Protein: | 32 g. | Sodium: | 977 mg. |
| Carbohydrate: | 14 g. | Cholesterol: | 72 mg. |

## Southwestern Supper
*6 servings*

---

*Beef Fajitas*
*Sautéed Peppers & Onions*
*Fresh Tomato Salsa*
*Cheese-topped Refried Beans*
*Jicama Salad with Lime-Honey Dressing*
*Orange Rum Soufflés*

---

### Time Management

**The day before:** Marinate steak in refrigerator. • Prepare and refrigerate soufflés. • Mix salsa and salad dressing; refrigerate.

**Early in the day:** Thaw guacamole in refrigerator. • Cut up and chill vegetables for Jicama Salad and Sautéed Peppers & Onions.

**About 30 minutes before serving:** Grill or broil steak conventionally while you microwave peppers and onions and refried beans. • Soften tortillas and assemble fajitas. • Toss salad just before serving. • Garnish soufflés before serving.

## Sautéed Peppers ▶ & Onions

1 medium green pepper, cut into thin strips
1 medium red pepper, cut into thin strips
1 medium red onion, thinly sliced, separated into rings
1 large clove garlic, cut into slivers
1 tablespoon vegetable oil

6 servings

In 2-quart casserole, combine all ingredients. Cover. Microwave at High for 5½ to 7 minutes, or until peppers are tender-crisp, stirring once or twice. Serve as accompaniment to fajitas.

| Per Serving: | |
| --- | --- |
| Calories: | 36 |
| Protein: | 1 g. |
| Carbohydrate: | 3 g. |
| Fat: | 2 g. |
| Sodium: | 2 mg. |
| Cholesterol: | — |

## Fresh Tomato Salsa ▶

2 cups seeded chopped tomatoes
¾ cup chopped onion
1 can (4 oz.) chopped green chilies, drained
1½ teaspoons dried cilantro leaves
¾ teaspoon salt
¼ teaspoon freshly ground pepper
Tortilla chips

6 servings

In medium mixing bowl, combine all ingredients, except tortilla chips. Mix well. Serve as accompaniment to fajitas. Garnish each serving with a tortilla chip.

| Per Serving: | |
| --- | --- |
| Calories: | 23 |
| Protein: | 1 g. |
| Carbohydrate: | 5 g. |
| Fat: | — |
| Sodium: | 439 mg. |
| Cholesterol: | — |

## Beef Fajitas ▶

**Marinade:**

¼ cup vegetable oil
¼ cup lime juice
2 tablespoons soy sauce
¼ teaspoon ground cumin
¼ teaspoon freshly ground pepper
⅛ teaspoon crushed red pepper flakes

2-lb. beef flank steak, about 1 inch thick, trimmed
12 flour tortillas (8-inch)
1 recipe Sautéed Peppers & Onions (left)
1 recipe Fresh Tomato Salsa (left)
  Sour cream
1 pkg. (6 oz.) frozen avocado guacamole, defrosted

6 servings

Up to 2 hours before, combine all marinade ingredients in 12 × 8-inch baking dish. Mix well. Add steak, turning to coat. Cover with plastic wrap. Chill, turning steak over occasionally. Remove steak from marinade; discard marinade. Place steak under conventional broiler 5 inches from heat or place on grill over medium heat. Broil or grill 18 to 20 minutes, or until desired doneness, turning once. Slice steak crosswise into ¼-inch strips. Cover to keep warm. Set aside.

Place six tortillas between 2 dampened paper towels. Microwave at High for 1 to 1¼ minutes, or until tortillas are warm to the touch. Repeat with remaining tortillas. Place about 3 strips of steak on each tortilla; top with Sautéed Peppers & Onions. Fold up from bottom. Fold in sides and secure with wooden pick, leaving top open. Top with Fresh Tomato Salsa, sour cream and guacamole.

| Per Serving: | |
| --- | --- |
| Calories: | 564 |
| Protein: | 35 g. |
| Carbohydrate: | 40 g. |
| Fat: | 30 g. |
| Sodium: | 821 mg. |
| Cholesterol: | 86 mg. |

## Jicama Salad with Lime-Honey Dressing ▲

**Dressing:**

- 3 tablespoons vegetable oil
- 2 tablespoons lime juice
- 2 tablespoons honey
- 3 drops red pepper sauce

**Salad:**

- 2 cups torn red-tipped leaf lettuce
- 2 cups julienne jicama (2 × ¼-inch strips)
- 1 orange, peeled and sectioned
- ⅓ cup walnut halves

6 servings

In small mixing bowl, combine all dressing ingredients. Mix well. Set aside. In large mixing bowl or salad bowl, combine all salad ingredients. Before serving, pour dressing over salad. Toss gently. Serve immediately.

| Per Serving: | | | |
|---|---|---|---|
| Calories: | 204 | Fat: | 15 g. |
| Protein: | 3 g. | Sodium: | 4 mg. |
| Carbohydrate: | 17 g. | Cholesterol: | — |

## Cheese-topped Refried Beans

1 can (16 oz.) refried beans
1 can (16 oz.) pinto beans, drained
1 can (4 oz.) chopped green chilies
2 tablespoons taco sauce
1 cup shredded Colby and Monterey Jack cheese
2 tablespoons sliced green onion

6 servings

In 2-quart casserole, combine refried beans, pinto beans, chilies and taco sauce. Mix well. Cover. Microwave at High for 6 to 8 minutes, or until hot, stirring once. Sprinkle with cheese. Re-cover. Microwave at High for 1 to 1½ minutes, or until cheese is melted. Sprinkle with green onion.

Per Serving:

| | | | |
|---|---|---|---|
| Calories: | 219 | Fat: | 7 g. |
| Protein: | 13 g. | Sodium: | 638 mg. |
| Carbohydrate: | 27 g. | Cholesterol: | 18 mg. |

## Orange Rum Soufflés

⅓ cup flaked coconut
6 egg whites
4 egg yolks
1 cup sugar, divided
2 tablespoons dark rum
2 tablespoons water
1 tablespoon grated orange
   peel
½ cup fresh orange juice
1 envelope (0.25 oz.)
   unflavored gelatin
4 drops yellow food coloring
2 drops red food coloring
¼ teaspoon cream of tartar
2 cups prepared whipped
   topping

6 servings

| Per Serving: | | | |
|---|---|---|---|
| Calories: | 282 | Fat: | 8 g. |
| Protein: | 7 g. | Sodium: | 76 mg. |
| Carbohydrate: | 42 g. | Cholesterol: | 184 mg. |

## How to Microwave Orange Rum Soufflés

**Sprinkle** coconut in 9-inch pie plate. Microwave at High for 3 to 4 minutes, or until lightly browned, tossing with fork every 30 seconds. Set aside. Place egg whites in large mixing bowl. Set aside. Place egg yolks in medium mixing bowl.

**Add** ⅔ cup sugar, the rum, water, orange peel, orange juice and gelatin to egg yolks. Mix well. Microwave at 50% (Medium) for 7 to 10 minutes, or until mixture thickens slightly, stirring with whisk 2 or 3 times. Add food coloring. Mix well.

**Place** bowl with hot mixture in larger bowl containing 1 to 2 inches ice water. Chill both bowls 15 minutes, or until mixture is very cold, but not set. Beat egg whites and cream of tartar at high speed of electric mixer until foamy.

**Add** remaining ⅓ cup sugar gradually to egg whites while continuing to beat. Beat until mixture forms stiff peaks. Fold whipped topping into egg white mixture. Add 1 cup egg white mixture to gelatin mixture.

**Beat** at medium speed of electric mixer until blended, about 1 minute. Return gelatin mixture to egg white mixture and gently fold to combine.

**Spoon** mixture evenly into each of six (6-oz.) ramekins or custard cups, mounding at least 1 inch higher than rim of ramekin. Chill at least 5 hours or overnight. Garnish with toasted coconut.

## Pasta Party
### 6-8 servings

*Fettucini with Fresh Mushrooms & Parsley*
*Sicilian Red Sauce*
*Venetian Seafood Sauce      Genoa Pesto Sauce*
*Romaine Salad with Parmesan Peppercorn Dressing*
*Bread Sticks\*      Spumoni Cake*

### Time Management

**The day before:** Microwave red sauce and seafood sauce; refrigerate. • Prepare and refrigerate pesto. • Prepare and refrigerate cake. • Wash romaine; wrap in dampened paper towels and refrigerate. • Prepare and refrigerate salad dressing.

**One hour before serving:** Remove pesto from refrigerator; let stand at room temperature. • Slice mushrooms and snip parsley for fettucini. • Boil water for pasta conventionally while you microwave red sauce to reheat. • Keep red sauce warm while you cook pasta and reheat seafood sauce. • Toss salad just before serving. • To serve party buffet-style, place red sauce and seafood sauce on hot tray or over warmers.

## Venetian Seafood Sauce

⅓ cup margarine or butter
¼ cup finely chopped onion
¼ cup white wine
1 lb. bay scallops
⅓ cup all-purpose flour
1 teaspoon salt
¼ teaspoon white pepper
3 cups milk
1 cup half-and-half
¼ cup snipped fresh parsley
¼ to ½ teaspoon freshly grated nutmeg

6 to 8 servings

In 2-quart casserole, combine margarine and onion. Cover. Microwave at High for 2 to 3 minutes, or until onion is tender-crisp. Add wine. Re-cover. Microwave at High for 2½ to 3 minutes, or until onion is tender. Add scallops. Re-cover. Microwave at 70% (Medium High) for 4½ to 5½ minutes, or until scallops are firm and opaque, stirring twice. Remove scallops from liquid with slotted spoon. Set aside.

Stir flour, salt and pepper into liquid. Blend in milk and half-and-half. Stir with whisk until mixture is smooth. Microwave at High for 13 to 18 minutes, or until mixture thickens and bubbles, stirring 3 or 4 times. Add scallops, parsley and nutmeg. Mix well. Cool slightly. Cover and chill 4 hours or overnight. To serve, microwave at High for 8 to 10 minutes, or until sauce is hot, stirring once.

Per Serving:
| | | | |
|---|---|---|---|
| Calories: | 232 | Fat: | 13 g. |
| Protein: | 14 g. | Sodium: | 507 mg. |
| Carbohydrate: | 12 g. | Cholesterol: | 37 mg. |

## Sicilian Red Sauce

1 lb. bulk Italian sausage
½ cup finely chopped onion
⅓ cup thinly sliced carrot
⅓ cup thinly sliced celery
¼ cup olive oil
2 tablespoons margarine or butter
3 cloves garlic, minced
⅓ cup red wine
1 can (28 oz.) Italian plum tomatoes, cut up and undrained
1 can (6 oz.) tomato paste
1 teaspoon dried oregano leaves
1 teaspoon dried basil leaves
1 teaspoon freshly ground pepper
1 teaspoon salt

6 to 8 servings

Crumble sausage into 1-quart casserole. Microwave at High for 6 to 8 minutes, or until meat is no longer pink, stirring once or twice to break apart. Drain. Set aside. In 3-quart casserole, combine onion, carrot, celery, oil, margarine and garlic. Cover. Microwave at High for 5 to 6 minutes, or until vegetables are tender-crisp, stirring once.

Add wine. Re-cover. Microwave at High for 2 to 3½ minutes, or until vegetables are tender. Add remaining ingredients. Re-cover. Microwave at High for 9 to 11 minutes, or until mixture is hot. Stir in sausage. Re-cover. Microwave at High for 3 to 4 minutes, or until sauce is hot and flavors blend. Cool slightly. Cover and chill 4 hours or overnight. To serve, microwave at High for 6 to 8 minutes, or until hot, stirring once.

Per Serving:
| | |
|---|---|
| Calories: | 240 |
| Protein: | 7 g. |
| Carbohydrate: | 11 g. |
| Fat: | 18 g. |
| Sodium: | 981 mg. |
| Cholesterol: | 22 mg. |

## Genoa Pesto Sauce

4 cups packed fresh basil
   leaves
⅓ cup snipped fresh parsley
⅓ cup walnut halves
3 cloves garlic

¾ cup olive oil
½ teaspoon salt
¼ teaspoon freshly ground
   pepper
¾ cup grated Parmesan cheese

6 to 8 servings

In food processor or blender, place all ingredients except Parmesan cheese. Process until mixture forms paste. Transfer to medium mixing bowl. Stir in Parmesan cheese. Mix well. Cover and chill 4 hours or overnight. Remove from refrigerator 1 hour before serving. Serve at room temperature.

Per Serving:

| | | | |
|---|---|---|---|
| Calories: | 269 | Fat: | 27 g. |
| Protein: | 5 g. | Sodium: | 324 mg. |
| Carbohydrate: | 4 g. | Cholesterol: | 7 mg. |

## Fettucini with Fresh Mushrooms & Parsley

2 lbs. uncooked egg or spinach
   fettucini
8 oz. fresh mushrooms, sliced
½ cup snipped fresh parsley
¼ cup olive oil

16 servings

Prepare fettucini as directed on package. Rinse and drain. Place cooked fettucini in large serving bowl. Add remaining ingredients. Toss gently to combine.

Per Serving:

| | |
|---|---|
| Calories: | 244 |
| Protein: | 7 g. |
| Carbohydrate: | 43 g. |
| Fat: | 4 g. |
| Sodium: | 2 mg. |
| Cholesterol: | — |

## Spumoni Cake ▶

| | |
|---|---|
| 1 | pkg. (18¼ oz.) white cake mix |
| ½ | cup chopped maraschino cherries |
| ½ | teaspoon cherry extract |
| 6 | drops red food coloring |
| ½ | cup plus 1 tablespoon chopped pistachio nuts, divided |
| 6 | drops green food coloring |
| 1½ | cups whipping cream |
| 1 | carton (15 oz.) ricotta cheese |
| 1¼ | cups powdered sugar |
| 1½ | teaspoons vanilla |

12 servings

Per Serving:
| | |
|---|---|
| Calories: | 492 |
| Protein: | 9 g. |
| Carbohydrate: | 51 g. |
| Fat: | 29 g. |
| Sodium: | 229 mg. |
| Cholesterol: | 52 mg. |

## Romaine Salad with Parmesan Peppercorn Dressing ▲

| | | | |
|---|---|---|---|
| ⅓ | cup mayonnaise | 1½ | to 2 teaspoons coarsely ground pepper |
| ¼ | cup sour cream | | Dash salt |
| ¼ | cup buttermilk | 8 | to 10 cups torn romaine lettuce |
| ¼ | cup grated Parmesan cheese | | Seasoned croutons |

6 to 8 servings

In small bowl, combine all ingredients except lettuce and croutons. Mix well. Chill 4 hours or overnight. Just before serving, place romaine in large mixing bowl or salad bowl. Pour dressing over salad. Toss gently to coat. Garnish with croutons.

Per Serving:
| | | | |
|---|---|---|---|
| Calories: | 117 | Fat: | 10 g. |
| Protein: | 3 g. | Sodium: | 161 mg. |
| Carbohydrate: | 4 g. | Cholesterol: | 11 mg. |

## How to Make Spumoni Cake

**Heat** conventional oven to 350°F. Grease and flour two 8-inch round cake pans. Prepare cake mix as directed on package. Place one-half of batter (about 2¼ cups) in medium mixing bowl. Set aside. To remaining batter add maraschino cherries, cherry extract and red food coloring. Mix well.

**Spread** evenly in one prepared pan. To remaining batter, add ½ cup pistachio nuts and the green food coloring. Mix well. Spread evenly in remaining prepared pan. Bake at 350°F for 28 to 35 minutes, or until wooden pick inserted in center comes out clean. Cool 15 minutes. Remove from pans and cool at least 2 hours.

**Beat** whipping cream in large mixing bowl at high speed of electric mixer until soft peaks form. Set aside. In medium mixing bowl, combine ricotta cheese, sugar and vanilla. Mix well. Fold into whipped cream. Set aside. Using serrated knife, carefully slice cake layers horizontally in half to make 4 thin cake layers.

**Place** bottom of cherry cake layer on serving platter. Spread with about ½ cup frosting. Top with 1 pistachio layer. Spread with about ½ cup frosting. Repeat with remaining cake layers. Spread top and sides of cake with remaining frosting. Chill cake at least 2 hours or overnight. Garnish with remaining 1 tablespoon pistachio nuts.

## French Dinner
*8 servings*

Cold Brie Soup
Mushroom-stuffed Tenderloin à la Marsala
Sunny Artichoke Platter          Crusty French Bread*
Petite Croissants with Fresh Fruit & French Crème

### Time Management

**The night before:** Prepare and refrigerate soup. • Prepare French crème and fruit; refrigerate.

**About 1 hour before serving:** Heat conventional oven while preparing tenderloin. • While tenderloin roasts, prepare artichoke platter. • Assemble dessert just before serving.

## Cold Brie Soup

| | |
|---|---|
| 1 lb. Brie cheese | ¼ teaspoon dried marjoram |
| 1 cup ready-to-serve chicken broth | leaves |
| | Dash white pepper |
| 2½ cups half-and-half | 1 Granny Smith apple, thinly sliced |

8 servings

Cut rind from Brie. Discard rind. In 8-cup measure, combine Brie and chicken broth. Microwave at 50% (Medium) for 5 to 9 minutes, or until mixture can be stirred smooth with whisk, stirring twice. Stir in remaining ingredients, except apples. Beat well with whisk until smooth. Cover. Chill at least 4 hours or overnight. Serve topped with apple slices.

Per Serving:

| | | | |
|---|---|---|---|
| Calories: | 302 | Fat: | 25 g. |
| Protein: | 15 g. | Sodium: | 484 mg. |
| Carbohydrate: | 6 g. | Cholesterol: | 85 mg. |

## Mushroom-stuffed Tenderloin à la Marsala

2½ to 3½-lb. beef tenderloin
1 to 2 tablespoons Dijon mustard
1 cup sliced fresh mushrooms
2 tablespoons snipped fresh parsley
½ cup Marsala wine

8 servings

Heat conventional oven to 350°F. Lightly grease a 15½ × 10½-inch jelly roll pan. Set aside. Slice tenderloin horizontally about three-fourths through, forming long opening. Spread evenly with desired amount of mustard. Arrange mushroom slices in even layer over mustard. Sprinkle with parsley. Close opening. Tie with string at 1½-inch intervals. Place tenderloin on prepared pan. Spoon small amount of wine over tenderloin. Roast for 35 to 45 minutes, or until beef is desired doneness, basting with remaining wine every 15 minutes.

Per Serving:

| | | | |
|---|---|---|---|
| Calories: | 344 | Fat: | 17 g. |
| Protein: | 41 g. | Sodium: | 144 mg. |
| Carbohydrate: | 1 g. | Cholesterol: | 128 mg. |

## Sunny Artichoke Platter

¼ cup margarine or butter
2 tablespoons lemon juice
1 teaspoon capers
⅛ teaspoon dried thyme leaves
1 pkg. (12 oz.) fresh baby carrots
2 fresh artichokes
   Lemon juice
1 large tomato

8 servings

In 2-cup measure, microwave margarine at High for 1¼ to 1½ minutes, or until melted. Stir in lemon juice, capers and thyme. Set aside. Peel and trim carrots. Trim stems close to base of each artichoke. Cut 1 inch off tops and trim ends off each leaf. Cut each artichoke lengthwise into fourths. Remove some of the center leaves and scrape out choke from each piece. Brush with lemon juice to prevent discoloration. Arrange carrots and artichoke pieces around outside edge of 12-inch platter. Spoon about 2 tablespoons caper mixture over vegetables. Cover with plastic wrap. Microwave at High for 8 to 12 minutes, or until vegetables are tender. Cut tomato into 8 wedges, leaving wedges connected at base. Place in center of vegetables and allow wedges to open up. Drizzle with remaining caper mixture.

| Per Serving: | | | |
|---|---|---|---|
| Calories: | 86 | Fat: | 6 g. |
| Protein: | 1 g. | Sodium: | 106 mg. |
| Carbohydrate: | 8 g. | Cholesterol: | — |

## Petite Croissants with Fresh Fruit & French Crème

### French Crème:

½ cup sour cream

½ cup whipping cream

2 pkgs. (6 oz. each) frozen petite croissants (12 croissants)

6 cups fresh strawberries, sliced

1 jar (10 oz.) strawberry jelly

2 tablespoons lemon juice

2 tablespoons orange-flavored liqueur (optional)

3 drops red food coloring (optional)

2 kiwifruit, peeled and sliced

12 servings

| Per Serving: | |
|---|---|
| Calories: | 266 |
| Protein: | 4 g. |
| Carbohydrate: | 38 g. |
| Fat: | 12 g. |
| Sodium: | 104 mg. |
| Cholesterol: | 18 mg. |

## How to Microwave Petite Croissants with Fresh Fruit & French Crème

**Combine** sour cream and whipping cream in small mixing bowl. Mix well. Cover with plastic wrap. Let stand at room temperature for about 8 hours to thicken. Chill 4 hours.

**Heat** conventional oven to 325°F. Slice each croissant in half crosswise. Place croissants on baking sheet. Bake for 6 to 7 minutes, or until golden brown. Set aside.

**Place** strawberries in medium mixing bowl. Set aside. In 2-cup measure, microwave jelly at High for 3 to 4 minutes, or until jelly is melted and can be stirred smooth, stirring once or twice.

**Add** lemon juice, liqueur and food coloring. Mix well. Pour jelly mixture over strawberries. Add kiwi slices. Toss gently to combine.

**Place** 1 croissant on dessert plate; fill with ½ cup strawberry mixture. Top with 1 heaping tablespoon of French crème. Repeat with remaining croissants, fruit and crème.

## It's a Dinner Party
### 6 servings

Veal Scallops with Pistachio Butter     Alfredo Spaghetti Squash
Pear & Walnut Salad     Decadent Chocolate Torte

### Time Management

**The day before or early in the day:** Prepare torte.

**About 45 minutes before serving:** Microwave sauce for pears and butter for veal. • Microwave squash and sauce. • Microwave pears and assemble salad. • Sauté veal conventionally.

## Veal Scallops with Pistachio Butter

¼ cup butter, plus 2 to 3
   tablespoons butter, divided
1 tablespoon chopped
   pistachio nuts
1 tablespoon snipped fresh
   parsley
⅓ cup all-purpose flour
¼ teaspoon salt
⅛ teaspoon white pepper
6 veal scallops (3 to 4 oz.
   each), about ¼ inch thick

6 servings

In small mixing bowl, microwave ¼ cup butter at 30% (Medium Low) for 15 to 30 seconds, or until softened, checking once. Stir in pistachios and parsley. Set aside. In shallow dish, combine flour, salt and pepper. In medium skillet, melt 2 tablespoons butter conventionally over medium-high heat. Dip veal scallops in flour mixture, coating both sides. Cook veal scallops about 1 to 2 minutes on each side, or until light golden brown, adding remaining butter to skillet, if necessary. Serve each cutlet topped with a dollop of pistachio butter.

Per Serving:

| | | | |
|---|---|---|---|
| Calories: | 334 | Fat: | 24 g. |
| Protein: | 24 g. | Sodium: | 262 mg. |
| Carbohydrate: | 6 g. | Cholesterol: | 117 mg. |

## Alfredo Spaghetti Squash

1 large spaghetti squash
   (about 3½ lbs.)
3 tablespoons margarine or
   butter
¼ cup sliced green onions
1 tablespoon all-purpose flour
⅛ teaspoon fennel seed
1 cup half-and-half
½ cup grated Parmesan cheese
1 large tomato, seeded and
   chopped

6 servings

Pierce squash rind deeply several times to allow steam to escape. Place squash on paper towel in microwave oven. Microwave at High for 10 to 15 minutes, or until rind begins to soften, turning over once. Cut squash in half crosswise. Cover face of each half with plastic wrap. Microwave at High for 9 to 13 minutes, or until tender. Let stand for 5 minutes. Scoop out and discard seeds and fibers. Twist away long strands of flesh with fork. Arrange on large platter. Cover to keep warm.

In 4-cup measure, combine margarine and onions. Microwave at High for 1 to 2 minutes, or until onion is tender-crisp. Stir in flour and fennel seed. Blend in half-and-half. Microwave at High for 2 to 4 minutes, or until mixture thickens and bubbles, stirring once. Stir in Parmesan cheese. Spoon over squash. Top with tomatoes.

Per Serving:

| | | | |
|---|---|---|---|
| Calories: | 214 | Fat: | 14 g. |
| Protein: | 6 g. | Sodium: | 272 mg. |
| Carbohydrate: | 17 g. | Cholesterol: | 22 mg. |

133

## Pear & Walnut Salad ▲

2 cans (16 oz. each) pear
  halves in light syrup
1 tablespoon cornstarch
2 teaspoons packed brown
  sugar
¼ teaspoon ground cinnamon
  Dash ground cloves
  Dash salt
  Leaf lettuce
1½ cups walnut halves

6 servings

Drain pears, reserving 1 cup pear liquid. Set pears aside. In 2-cup measure, combine cornstarch, brown sugar, cinnamon, cloves and salt. Blend in reserved pear liquid. Microwave at High for 2 to 5 minutes, or until mixture is thickened and translucent, stirring once or twice. Set aside. Place pear halves in 9-inch pie plate. Cover with wax paper. Microwave at High for 2 to 3 minutes, or until hot. Line individual salad plates with lettuce. Arrange pear halves evenly on lettuce. Top with walnuts. Drizzle 2 to 3 tablespoons pear liquid over each salad.

Per Serving:
| | | | |
|---|---|---|---|
| Calories: | 293 | Fat: | 19 g. |
| Protein: | 5 g. | Sodium: | 34 mg. |
| Carbohydrate: | 32 g. | Cholesterol: | — |

# ◀ Decadent Chocolate Torte

| | |
|---|---|
| 1 | pkg. (8 oz.) unsweetened chocolate, divided |
| ⅔ | cup plus 2 tablespoons margarine or butter, divided |
| 1 | cup sugar, divided |

| | |
|---|---|
| 1¼ | cups ground blanched almonds, divided |
| ½ | cup all-purpose flour |
| 3 | eggs, separated |
| ¼ | teaspoon almond extract |
| ½ | cup powdered sugar, sifted |
| 2 | tablespoons water |

Per Serving:

| | |
|---|---|
| Calories: | 382 |
| Protein: | 6 g. |
| Carbohydrate: | 33 g. |
| Fat: | 29 g. |
| Sodium: | 160 mg. |
| Cholesterol: | 69 mg. |

12 servings

## How to Make Decadent Chocolate Torte

**Heat** conventional oven to 350°F. Grease and flour 9-inch round cake pan. Set aside. In medium mixing bowl, combine 6 oz. chocolate, ⅔ cup margarine and ¾ cup sugar.

**Microwave** at 50% (Medium) for 4 to 5½ minutes, or until mixture can be stirred smooth, stirring 2 or 3 times. Stir in 1 cup ground almonds, the flour, egg yolks and extract. Mix well. Set aside.

**Beat** egg whites in medium mixing bowl at high speed of electric mixer until foamy. Gradually add remaining ¼ cup sugar, beating until stiff peaks form. Fold egg whites into chocolate batter.

**Spread** batter in prepared pan. Bake for 30 minutes, or until wooden pick inserted in center comes out clean. Let cool for 10 minutes. Invert on serving plate. Cover and cool completely.

**Place** remaining 2 tablespoons margarine and 2 oz. chocolate in 2-cup measure. Microwave at 50% (Medium) for 1½ to 2½ minutes, or until margarine is melted and mixture can be stirred smooth.

**Stir** in powdered sugar. Stir in water. Stir with whisk until smooth. Pour over torte. Spread to coat top of cake, allowing glaze to run down sides. Decorate edges of torte with remaining ¼ cup ground almonds.

### *Dinner on Ice*
*6-8 servings*

---

*Chilled Cantaloupe Soup*

*Cold Sesame Chicken*     *Oriental Pasta & Vegetable Salad*

*Sesame Bread Sticks* *     *Almond Cookies*

---

### Time Management

**The day before:** Prepare and bake cookies. • Prepare salad; cover and refrigerate. • Microwave syrup; add melon. Cover and refrigerate. • Marinate chicken breasts. Cover and refrigerate.

**The evening before or early in the day:** Process cantaloupe-yogurt mixture; cover and refrigerate. • Microwave chicken; cover and refrigerate.

**Just before serving:** Place soup in serving bowls; garnish with lime. • Arrange chicken for serving; garnish with peanut-parsley mixture.

## Cold Sesame Chicken

4 bone-in whole chicken
   breasts (10 to 12 oz. each),
   split in half, skin removed
¼ cup soy sauce
2 tablespoons peanut oil
1 tablespoon white wine
½ teaspoon sesame oil
½ teaspoon sugar
1 clove garlic, minced
½ cup chopped peanuts
3 tablespoons snipped fresh
   parsley

6 to 8 servings

Place chicken breast halves in large plastic food-storage bag. Set aside. In 1-cup measure, combine soy sauce, peanut oil, wine, sesame oil, sugar and garlic. Mix well. Pour soy sauce mixture over chicken breasts. Chill at least 4 hours or overnight, turning chicken over once. Remove chicken breasts from marinade. Discard marinade.

Arrange 4 chicken breast halves on roasting rack, with meaty portions toward outside. Cover with wax paper. Microwave at High for 10 to 12 minutes, or until chicken near bone is no longer pink and juices run clear, rotating 2 or 3 times. Repeat with remaining chicken breast halves. Arrange cooked chicken breasts in even layer on serving platter. Cover. Chill at least 4 hours or overnight. In small bowl, combine peanuts and parsley. Before serving, sprinkle 1 tablespoon of peanut and parsley mixture over each chicken breast half.

| Per Serving: | |
| --- | --- |
| Calories: | 249 |
| Protein: | 38 g. |
| Carbohydrate: | 2 g. |
| Fat: | 9 g. |
| Sodium: | 230 mg. |
| Cholesterol: | 96 mg. |

## Chilled Cantaloupe Soup

2 cups water
1 cup sugar
2 tablespoons lemon juice
1 tablespoon crystallized ginger,
   finely chopped

1 medium cantaloupe, seeded,
   peeled and cut into 1-inch
   chunks (about 5 cups)
2 cartons (8 oz. each) French
   vanilla yogurt
8 thin slices lime

6 to 8 servings

In 2-quart casserole, combine water, sugar, lemon juice and ginger. Microwave at High for 5 to 7 minutes, or until sugar is dissolved, stirring twice. Add cantaloupe. Cover. Chill until cantaloupe mixture is cold, about 6 hours or overnight. In blender, place one-half cantaloupe mixture and 1 carton yogurt; process cantaloupe-yogurt mixture until smooth. Pour into large mixing bowl. Repeat with remaining cantaloupe mixture and yogurt. Cover. Chill until serving time. Garnish each serving with one lime slice.

| Per Serving: | | | |
| --- | --- | --- | --- |
| Calories: | 177 | Fat: | 1 g. |
| Protein: | 3 g. | Sodium: | 45 mg. |
| Carbohydrate: | 41 g. | Cholesterol: | 3 mg. |

## Oriental Pasta
## & Vegetable Salad

1 pkg. (10 oz.) frozen cut green
   beans
1 cup uncooked mostaccioli
2 cups fresh cauliflowerets
1 cup cherry tomatoes,
   quartered
1 cup sliced fresh mushrooms
½ cup diagonally sliced green
   onions, cut into 1-inch
   lengths
½ cup mayonnaise
2 tablespoons soy sauce
¾ teaspoon sesame oil
½ teaspoon Chinese hot oil
¼ teaspoon cayenne

6 to 8 servings

In 1-quart casserole, microwave
beans at High for 4 to 6 minutes,
or until defrosted, stirring 2 or 3
times to break apart. Drain. Set
aside. Prepare mostaccioli as directed on package. Rinse and
drain. In large mixing bowl, combine beans, cooked mostaccioli,
the cauliflowerets, tomatoes,
mushrooms and onions. Set aside.
In small mixing bowl, combine remaining ingredients. Beat with
whisk until combined. Pour mayonnaise mixture over vegetable
and pasta mixture. Toss to coat.
Chill salad at least 4 hours or
overnight.

Per Serving:
  Calories:                  169
  Protein:                   3 g.
  Carbohydrate:       14 g.
  Fat:                     12 g.
  Sodium:              345 mg.
  Cholesterol:         8 mg.

## Almond Cookies

| | |
|---|---|
| 1 | cup margarine or butter |
| ⅔ | cup powdered sugar |
| 1 | egg |
| 1 | teaspoon vanilla |
| ½ | teaspoon almond extract |
| 1 | teaspoon grated lemon peel |
| 2⅓ | cups all-purpose flour |
| ½ | teaspoon baking powder |
| 1 | egg yolk |
| 1 | tablespoon water |
| 24 | whole blanched almonds |

2 dozen cookies

Per Serving:
| | |
|---|---|
| Calories: | 144 |
| Protein: | 2 g. |
| Carbohydrate: | 13 g. |
| Fat: | 10 g. |
| Sodium: | 99 mg. |
| Cholesterol: | 23 mg. |

## How to Make Almond Cookies

**Heat** conventional oven to 350°F. In large mixing bowl, cream margarine and sugar at medium speed of electric mixer until light and fluffy. Add egg, vanilla, almond extract and lemon peel. Mix well. Add flour and baking powder; stir until blended. Set aside.

**Blend** egg yolk and water in small mixing bowl. Set aside. Shape dough into 1-inch balls; place 2 inches apart on ungreased cookie sheets. Flatten slightly with flat bottom of glass, rubbing glass over damp cloth to prevent sticking.

**Brush** tops of cookies lightly with egg mixture. Top each cookie with whole almond, pressing into dough slightly. Bake for 11 to 15 minutes, or until edges are light golden brown. Cool on wire rack.

139

## Grilled Ribs with Plum Barbecue Sauce

6  lbs. pork spare ribs, trimmed and cut into serving-size pieces
1  small onion, sliced and separated into rings
4  to 6 thin lemon slices
½  teaspoon salt
¼  teaspoon pepper

**Sauce:**
½  cup finely chopped onion
¼  cup vegetable oil
4  cloves garlic, minced
2  cups plum jam
½  cup honey
¼  cup red wine vinegar
2  teaspoons dry mustard
1  teaspoon ground ginger
½  teaspoon freshly ground pepper

6 to 8 servings

Heat conventional oven to 350°F. Arrange ribs, slightly overlapping, in large roasting pan. Sprinkle with onion and lemon slices, salt and pepper. Cover with foil. Bake 1 hour 20 minutes to 1 hour 30 minutes, or until ribs are tender. Set aside.

In 8-cup measure, combine onion, oil and garlic. Cover with plastic wrap. Microwave at High for 3 to 4 minutes, or until onion is tender, stirring once or twice. Add remaining ingredients. Mix well. Microwave at High, uncovered, for 4 to 5 minutes, or until mixture is hot and just begins to boil, stirring twice.

Grill ribs over medium-high heat for 11 to 16 minutes, or until deep golden brown, brushing with sauce and turning several times during grilling. Serve ribs with remaining sauce.

| Per Serving: | | | |
|---|---|---|---|
| Calories: | 867 | Fat: | 47 g. |
| Protein: | 40 g. | Sodium: | 270 mg. |
| Carbohydrate: | 73 g. | Cholesterol: | 161 mg. |

## New Potato & Avocado Salad

 2 lbs. whole new potatoes (about 15 potatoes)
¼ cup water
½ cup chopped red onion

### Dressing:

½ cup mayonnaise
½ cup sour cream
 1 tablespoon lemon juice
 1 tablespoon sugar
½ teaspoon salt
¼ teaspoon white pepper

 2 tablespoons lemon juice
 2 avocados, peeled and sliced (about 2 cups)
 1 large cucumber, cut in half lengthwise, seeded and coarsely chopped (about 2 cups)
 1 cup sliced radishes

6 to 8 servings

Pierce potatoes with fork. In 3-quart casserole, place potatoes and water. Cover. Microwave at High for 13 to 18 minutes, or just until tender, rearranging once. Let cool slightly. Slice potatoes into ½-inch slices. Place potato slices and red onion in large mixing bowl or salad bowl. Set aside.

In small mixing bowl, combine all dressing ingredients. Mix well. Add dressing to potatoes and onion. Toss gently to coat. Cover with plastic wrap. Chill at least 4 hours or overnight. Just before serving, place 2 tablespoons lemon juice into 9-inch pie plate. Dip each avocado slice in lemon juice. Add avocado, cucumber and radishes to potato mixture. Toss gently. Serve immediately.

| Per Serving: | |
|---|---|
| Calories: | 390 |
| Protein: | 7 g. |
| Carbohydrate | 43 g. |
| Fat: | 23 g. |
| Sodium: | 250 mg. |
| Cholesterol: | 15 mg. |

# Blueberry Sugar-crusted Cobbler

### Sauce:
½ cup honey
¼ teaspoon grated orange
    peel
2 tablespoons orange juice
    Dash ground allspice

### Filling:
1¼ cups sugar
¼ cup cornstarch
1 teaspoon grated orange
    peel
⅛ teaspoon ground allspice
2 pkgs. (16 oz. each) frozen
    blueberries
2 tablespoons orange juice

### Topping:
1 sheet frozen puff pastry,
    defrosted (half of
    17¼-oz. pkg.)
    Milk
2 tablespoons sugar

8 servings

Heat conventional oven to 350°F. In 2-cup measure, combine all sauce ingredients. Microwave at High for 30 seconds to 1 minute, or until hot, stirring once. Set aside to cool. In 3-quart casserole, combine all filling ingredients except orange juice. Mix well. Microwave at High for 17 to 30 minutes, or until mixture is thickened and translucent, stirring 3 or 4 times. Stir in orange juice. Spoon mixture into a shallow 2-quart baking dish. Cool 10 minutes.

Place puff pastry on lightly floured surface. Roll to 12-inch length. Brush lightly with milk. Sprinkle with sugar. Cut into ¾-inch strips. Arrange strips in lattice fashion over blueberry mixture, trimming to fit. Bake for 20 to 25 minutes, or until hot and bubbly and pastry is golden brown. Top cobbler with sauce and serve with ice cream, if desired.

| Per Serving: | | | |
|---|---|---|---|
| Calories: | 344 | Fat: | 5 g. |
| Protein: | 2 g. | Sodium: | 83 mg. |
| Carbohydrate: | 78 g. | Cholesterol: | — |

## Broiled Lamb Kabobs

### *Grecian Isles Dinner*
*6-8 servings*

*Broiled Lamb Kabobs*
*Tabbouleh-style Rice*
*Mint Chip Cheesecake*

#### Time Management

**The day before:** Marinate lamb in the refrigerator.

**The day before or early in the day:** Prepare cheesecake; refrigerate. • Prepare mint dessert sauce. Cover and set aside. • Cook brown rice. Cover and refrigerate.

**About 30 minutes before serving:** Skewer lamb cubes and lemon. • While lamb broils conventionally, prepare remaining ingredients for rice; assemble and microwave.

**Marinade:**
⅔ cup olive or vegetable oil
3 tablespoons lemon juice
1 tablespoon snipped fresh mint leaves or 1 teaspoon dried mint flakes
1 teaspoon dried oregano leaves

1 clove garlic, minced
½ teaspoon salt
¼ teaspoon pepper

3-lb. boneless leg of lamb, cut into 1½-inch cubes (about 40 cubes)
8 metal skewers, 10-inch
16 thin lemon slices

6 to 8 servings

In 1-cup measure, combine all marinade ingredients. Mix well. Place lamb cubes in large plastic food-storage bag. Pour marinade mixture over lamb. Close bag. Refrigerate at least 12 hours or overnight, turning bag occasionally. On each skewer, thread 1 lamb cube. Wrap 1 lemon slice around 1 lamb cube, and skewer. Add another lamb cube and 1 more lamb cube wrapped with lemon slice. Finish with lamb cube. Do not pack tightly. Arrange kabobs in even layer on conventional broiler pan. Broil kabobs 3 inches from heat for 16 to 20 minutes, or until desired doneness, turning kabobs over once.

| Per Serving: | | | |
|---|---|---|---|
| Calories: | 280 | Fat: | 13 g. |
| Protein: | 37 g. | Sodium: | 124 mg. |
| Carbohydrate: | 1 g. | Cholesterol: | 128 mg. |

## Tabbouleh-style Rice

¼ cup olive or vegetable oil
2 tablespoons lemon juice
1 clove garlic, minced
½ teaspoon salt
¼ teaspoon pepper
4 cups cooked brown rice
1 medium cucumber, cut in half
   lengthwise, seeded and
   sliced (¼-inch slices)
1 large tomato, seeded and
   chopped (about 1 cup)
½ cup snipped fresh parsley
⅓ cup sliced green onions
¼ cup sliced black olives
2 tablespoons snipped fresh
   mint leaves or 2 teaspoons
   dried mint flakes

6 to 8 servings

In 1-cup measure, combine oil, lemon juice, garlic, salt and pepper. Mix well. Set aside. In 2-quart casserole, microwave cooked brown rice at High for 2 to 6 minutes, or until just warm, stirring once. Add oil mixture and remaining ingredients. Toss gently to combine. Serve warm.

Per Serving:
| | |
|---|---|
| Calories: | 194 |
| Protein: | 3 g. |
| Carbohydrate: | 28 g. |
| Fat: | 8 g. |
| Sodium: | 174 mg. |
| Cholesterol: | — |

## Mint Chip Cheesecake

**Crust:**
¼ cup margarine or butter
1 cup finely crushed chocolate
   wafer crumbs (about 20
   wafers)

**Filling:**
3 pkgs. (8 oz. each) cream
   cheese
1 cup sugar

2 eggs
3 tablespoons crème de
   menthe syrup
2 tablespoons all-purpose flour
1 cup mini semisweet
   chocolate chips

**Sauce:**
½ cup crème de menthe syrup
¼ cup light corn syrup

12 servings

In 9-inch round baking dish, microwave margarine at High for 1¼ to 1½ minutes, or until melted. Stir in wafer crumbs. Mix well. Press mixture firmly against bottom of dish. Microwave at High for 1½ to 2 minutes, or until set, rotating dish once. Set aside.

In 8-cup measure, microwave cream cheese at 50% (Medium) for 2½ to 5 minutes, or until softened. Add remaining filling ingredients, except chocolate chips. Beat at medium speed of electric mixer until well blended. Stir in chocolate chips. Pour filling over prepared crust. Place dish on saucer in microwave oven. Microwave at High for 3 minutes. Microwave at 50% (Medium) for 7 to 18 minutes longer, or until center is almost set, rotating dish twice (filling becomes firm as it cools). Refrigerate at least 8 hours or overnight. In 1-cup measure, combine sauce ingredients. Top each serving with 1 tablespoon sauce.

Per Serving:
| | | | |
|---|---|---|---|
| Calories: | 492 | Fat: | 31 g. |
| Protein: | 7 g. | Sodium: | 251 mg. |
| Carbohydrate: | 52 g. | Cholesterol: | 111 mg. |

## Tropical Sweet Potato & Pineapple Kabobs ▲

8 wooden skewers, 6-inch
1 red pepper, cut into 16 chunks
4 fresh pineapple slices, about
   ¾-inch slices, each cut into
   fourths
1 can (23 oz.) sweet potatoes,
   drained
3 tablespoons gravy (opposite)

8 servings

On each skewer, thread 1 red pepper chunk, 1 pineapple wedge, 1 sweet potato, 1 pineapple wedge and 1 red pepper chunk. Repeat with remaining ingredients. Arrange kabobs in even layer in 10-inch square casserole. Drizzle with gravy. Cover with plastic wrap. Microwave at High for 3 to 5 minutes, or until hot, rotating once. Arrange kabobs around Calypso Pork Roast, if desired.

| Per Serving: | | | |
|---|---|---|---|
| Calories: | 82 | Fat: | 2 g. |
| Protein: | 1 g. | Sodium: | 8 mg. |
| Carbohydrate: | 16 g. | Cholesterol: | 1 mg. |

Calypso Pork Roast with Gravy
Tropical Sweet Potato & Pineapple Kabobs
Caribbean Cabbage Salad        Coconut Cream Parfaits

### Time Management

**Early in the day:** Prepare and chill coconut parfaits.

**About 2½ to 2¾ hours before serving:** Heat conventional oven; season roast. • While pork roasts, prepare and chill salad; assemble kabobs. • Microwave gravy while roast stands. Brush kabobs with gravy and microwave just before serving.

## Calypso Pork Roast

4 to 5-lb. boneless pork loin
   roast
2 large cloves garlic, each cut
   into 8 pieces
¾ cup packed dark brown
   sugar
1 teaspoon ground ginger
½ teaspoon ground cinnamon
½ teaspoon salt
¼ teaspoon freshly ground
   pepper
2 tablespoons dark rum
1 cup pineapple juice
½ cup water

   **8 servings**

Heat conventional oven to 325°F. Cut sixteen 1-inch slits in pork roast. Insert garlic pieces. Place roast, fattiest-side-up, on rack in large roasting pan. Insert meat thermometer. Roast for 1 hour 30 minutes. In small mixing bowl, combine brown sugar, ginger, cinnamon, salt and pepper. Mix well. Add rum. Mix well. Remove roast from conventional oven. Spread roast evenly with brown sugar mixture. Add pineapple juice and water to bottom of roasting pan. Continue roasting for 30 to 50 minutes longer, or until internal temperature registers 165°F. Let roast stand for 10 minutes before carving. Strain and reserve drippings for gravy (below).

Per Serving:

| | | | |
|---|---|---|---|
| Calories: | 499 | Fat: | 18 g. |
| Protein: | 55 g. | Sodium: | 275 mg. |
| Carbohydrate: | 25 g. | Cholesterol: | 167 mg. |

## Gravy

2 cups reserved drippings
   (above)
1 tablespoon plus 1½
   teaspoons cornstarch

   **About 2 cups**

Place drippings in 4-cup measure. Place cornstarch in small bowl. Add small amount of drippings to cornstarch. Stir until mixture is smooth. Add back to remaining drippings, stirring with whisk until smooth. Microwave at High for 4 to 5 minutes, or until mixture is thickened and translucent, stirring twice. Reserve 3 tablespoons gravy for Tropical Sweet Potato & Pineapple Kabobs (opposite).

Per Serving:

| | | | |
|---|---|---|---|
| Calories: | 128 | Fat: | 14 g. |
| Protein: | — | Sodium: | — |
| Carbohydrate: | 1 g. | Cholesterol: | 13 mg. |

## Caribbean Cabbage Salad

- 1 cup mayonnaise
- 1 tablespoon lemon juice
- 1 tablespoon sugar
- ⅛ teaspoon ground nutmeg
- 8 cups shredded cabbage
- 1 cup salted cashew pieces
- 2 medium bananas, sliced

8 servings

In small mixing bowl, combine mayonnaise, lemon juice, sugar and nutmeg. Mix well. In large mixing bowl or salad bowl, combine cabbage and cashew pieces. Add mayonnaise mixture. Mix well. Cover and chill up to 2 hours before serving. Fold in bananas. Serve immediately.

| Per Serving: | | | |
|---|---|---|---|
| Calories: | 348 | Fat: | 30 g. |
| Protein: | 4 g. | Sodium: | 281 mg. |
| Carbohydrate: | 19 g. | Cholesterol: | 16 mg. |

# Coconut Cream Parfaits

2 pkgs. (3⅛ oz. each) coconut cream pudding and pie filling
4 cups milk
½ cup flaked coconut
1 can (20 oz.) pineapple chunks, drained
½ cup cashew pieces
    Prepared whipped topping
8 maraschino cherries with stems

8 servings

Place pudding in 8-cup measure. Blend in milk. Microwave at High for 11 to 20 minutes, or until pudding thickens and bubbles, stirring after first 3 minutes and then every 2 minutes. Place plastic wrap directly on surface of pudding. Chill about 4 hours, or until completely cool.

Sprinkle coconut in even layer in 9-inch pie plate. Microwave at High for 4 to 6 minutes, or until lightly browned, tossing with fork after first minute and then every 30 seconds. Set aside.

In each of eight (8-oz.) parfait or wine glasses, layer ¼ cup pudding mixture, 1 tablespoon toasted coconut, 4 or 5 chunks of pineapple, 1 tablespoon of cashew pieces and ¼ cup pudding mixture. Garnish each parfait with dollop of whipped topping and a cherry.

Per Serving:
| | |
|---|---|
| Calories: | 263 |
| Protein: | 7 g. |
| Carbohydrate: | 40 g. |
| Fat: | 10 g. |
| Sodium: | 173 mg. |
| Cholesterol: | 10 mg. |

## Vegetables in Ginger Butter ▶

¼ cup margarine or butter
½ teaspoon grated fresh
   gingerroot
2 teaspoons lemon juice
¼ teaspoon salt
   Dash pepper

4 cups fresh broccoli flowerets
2 cups fresh cauliflowerets
1 cup julienne carrots (2 × ¼-
   inch strips)
1 medium onion, cut into 8
   wedges

6 servings

In 3-quart casserole, combine margarine and gingerroot. Microwave at High for 1¼ to 1½ minutes, or until margarine is melted. Stir in lemon juice, salt and pepper. Add vegetables. Toss to coat. Cover. Microwave at High for 9 to 14 minutes, or until vegetables are tender-crisp, stirring once or twice.

| Per Serving: | | | |
|---|---|---|---|
| Calories: | 106 | Fat: | 8 g. |
| Protein: | 3 g. | Sodium: | 206 mg. |
| Carbohydrate: | 8 g. | Cholesterol: | — |

## Sesame Pasta ▶

1 lb. uncooked angel hair
   spaghetti or capellini
¼ cup sesame oil

¼ cup vegetable oil
2 tablespoons soy sauce

6 servings

Prepare angel hair spaghetti as directed on package. Rinse and drain. Add remaining ingredients. Toss to coat.

| Per Serving: | | | |
|---|---|---|---|
| Calories: | 444 | Fat: | 19 g. |
| Protein: | 10 g. | Sodium: | 345 mg. |
| Carbohydrate: | 57 g. | Cholesterol: | — |

## Bangkok Shrimp Sauté ▶

**Marinade:**
2 tablespoons soy sauce
1 tablespoon cream of
   coconut
¼ teaspoon garlic powder
⅛ teaspoon crushed red
   pepper flakes

1½ lbs. large shrimp, shelled
   and deveined

**Sauce:**
½ cup creamy peanut butter
¼ cup plus 2 tablespoons
   cream of coconut
2 tablespoons soy sauce
½ teaspoon crushed red
   pepper flakes
¼ cup whipping cream

2 tablespoons vegetable oil
   Coarsely chopped seeded
   cucumber
   Sliced green onions

6 servings

In medium mixing bowl, combine all marinade ingredients. Add shrimp. Toss to coat. Set aside. In 4-cup measure, combine all sauce ingredients, except cream. Microwave at High for 30 seconds to 1 minute, or until warm. Stir until smooth. Stir in cream. Set aside. In large skillet, heat oil conventionally over medium-high heat. Add shrimp and marinade. Stir-fry until shrimp are opaque. Reduce heat to low. Gradually stir in sauce. Cook for 2 to 3 minutes, or until mixture thickens slightly, stirring constantly. Before serving, sprinkle with cucumber and green onions.

| Per Serving: | |
|---|---|
| Calories: | 355 |
| Protein: | 25 g. |
| Carbohydrate: | 8 g. |
| Fat: | 26 g. |
| Sodium: | 874 mg. |
| Cholesterol: | 143 mg. |

## Fresh Pineapple Sorbet

2 cups water
2 cups sugar
1 fresh pineapple (about 3½ to 4 lbs.)

8 servings

| Per Serving: | |
|---|---|
| Calories: | 234 |
| Protein: | — |
| Carbohydrate: | 60 g. |
| Fat: | — |
| Sodium: | 1 mg. |
| Cholesterol: | — |

## How to Microwave Fresh Pineapple Sorbet

**Combine** water and sugar in 8-cup measure. Microwave at High for 6 to 7 minutes, or until sugar is dissolved, stirring twice. Set aside.

**Cut** pineapple in half lengthwise, leaving leafy portions attached. With thin, flexible knife, loosen and remove fruit, leaving ½-inch shells. Place each shell in large plastic food-storage bag. Place in freezer.

**Cut** and discard core from fruit. Place fruit in blender or food processor. Process until smooth (about 2 cups puréed fruit). Add puréed pineapple to sugar-water mixture. Stir to combine.

**Pour** mixture into 12 × 8-inch baking dish. Freeze for 4 to 6 hours, or until firm, stirring once every hour to break apart mixture. Cover with plastic wrap and freeze overnight, if desired.

**Let** sorbet stand at room temperature for 5 to 10 minutes to soften. Using an ice cream scoop, form mixture into balls. Serve sorbet from frozen pineapple shells.

# Index